WALKING WITHOUT
FEAR

Letting Go of Self and Living in the Joy of What Is

KELLAN FLUCKIGER

RED AUSSIE
— P U B L I S H I N G —

Published in Phoenix, Arizona, by Red Aussie Publishing
22424 S Ellsworth Loop Rd
Unit 898
Queen Creek, AZ 85142
Contact the Publisher: RedAussiePublishing@gmail.com
Or www.RedAussiePublishing.com
Contact the author:
www.KellanFluckiger.com

Printed in the United States of America
First Printing 2020
First Edition 2020

ISBN: 978-1-9994945-5-1

10 9 8 7 6 5 4 3 2 1

Red Aussie Publishing CEO: Joy Fluckiger
Cover Art & Layout: Joy Fluckiger

WALKING WITHOUT
FEAR

RED AUSSIE

— PUBLISHING —

TABLE OF CONTENTS

FOREWORD

I met Kellan a few years ago at an event where I spoke. Often, I do some laser coaching during presentations, and Kellan volunteered for this opportunity.

He shared some of his struggles, and my intuition came as it usually does. I gave him what I knew, and it was powerful and meaningful for him. How do I know? I saw the emotion and truth in tears.

Since that time, Kellan has been on a journey, nothing short of amazing. He is a coach and has a worldwide client base, but that's not the powerful part.

In the years since we met, Kellan's journey has taken him to the brink of death and back again to life. He had one of those "near-death" experiences we read about, and few of us have. He was in a coma for 2 ½ weeks battling an often fatal double pneumonia superbug infection. He survived and chose to come back to this life.

A dark night of the soul, conversations with God and all the rest, epiphany, enlightenment, however you describe it, are the substance from which much deep motivation and truth-telling emerge.

After this, he has written several more books to share the powerful truths he knows with those who are seeking. Like me, he encourages people to dream big, claim their rightful divinity, and blossom in creativity in the service of those they meet.

I followed his journey through video and occasional messages. We met again face to face in Poland, where I was again speaking on my passion and love. Dream big, dare boldly and make impossible things happen.

We joyfully chatted, and he told me about this latest book, *Walking Without Fear*. It's the second of a trilogy that comes from the experiences he had on the "other side."

Kellan is on a mission to invite every person into their greatest selves. Not in some esoteric way that is weird. Not just some few who are on the fringes, but every person who has that feeling that there is something more. I am one of those, so are you.

What I know for sure, is that Kellan gives you truth here, and invites you to explore what is truly possible for you, here, now. If you are willing, dive in and write these words in your heart and on your wall. I know I will.

Marcia Wieder
CEO, Dream University® and best-selling author
Lisbon, Portugal
January 2020

"The moment you realize that your beliefs control everything, life begins and your possibilities explode."

Kellan Fluckiger

INTRODUCTION

We all have fear. Fear is as pervasive as air. Even if there was no air, there would still be fear until the absence of air killed us. Then the fear would end.

I'm not talking about fears. Specific individual things that freak us out. You know, fear of the dark, fear of small places, fear of spiders. Those are at least tangible and make sense in some way. I'm talking about raw, unnamed, vague, but overpowering fear.

Fear is the universal limiter. It has blocked more dreams, limited more vision, and ended more progress than anything else in human history. It is the master destroyer of possibility.

I lived all my life, at least until I was 54, with fear – the constant, paralyzing, monster under the bed, debilitating fear. It led me to very the darkest places, including attempted suicide.

The story of my decades-long battle with depression, fear, and the terrible consequences are not the subject of this book. That story is in "Tight rope of Depression," for anyone interested in details.

Life is entirely different now. I no longer live with fear. It no longer controls any part of my thinking, feeling, or behavior in any way. Every day I draw breath, I am overwhelmed with gratitude because of the miraculous change.

The change came not by magic, but as the result of some very specific events and choices. Some involve divine manifestation or, in other words, connection with powers greater than we are.

We know those powers exist, and we often feel at a loss to know what they mean, how to access our "higher selves" and how to make good use of them.

This book exists for three reasons:

1.   I have something to share. After my "Near-Death" experience in the summer of 2018, I wrote *The Book of Context*, about one of three conversations between myself and God at the doorway between life and eternity. I thought my quota of astounding experiences was full. It wasn't. I'm writing this book to share what happened next, which gave me more information and power in living a productive and happy life.

2.   I want to explain the principles I learned. These have given me both a point of view and life experience without fear and full of opportunity and joy.

3.   I want to teach those who are ready and interested in how they can do the same for themselves. I want you to know it is possible to live without fear and have a successful and joyful life; every single day you draw breath.

When I wrote *The Book of Context*, I didn't expect there to be another volume. After more happened (described in this book), it was clear that there was more the story.

This book is part two of a trilogy. It is called the "Context" series. What's written here is powerful, relevant, and will benefit anyone with an open heart and a desire to grow.

The third book in the series will be published in fall 2020. Life gets sweeter every day, and I can't wait to share everything with you, so you, too, will walk without fear.

KELLAN FLUCKIGER

PROLOGUE

I finished speaking to the group and said, "Amen." It was not a religious gathering, and the word could be considered completely out of context, but it was absolutely appropriate for the occasion.

The room exploded. Every person was on their feet faster than I could think, and the applause was sustained and unrestrained. I had not expected such a response. In fact, I hadn't really expected anything.

I belonged to a mastermind of capable and powerful coaches who meet for three days, three times a year – this was the third meeting.

I missed the second meeting three months earlier because I spent most of June and part of July 2018, in the hospital. I was in the intensive care unit of the University of Alberta hospital. In the first two and a half weeks, I was in a coma and another couple of weeks in recovery.

During my time in the coma, I was not expected to live. I had a "Near-Death" experience. One of those things you never think will happen to you, but it did.

The second was in July, a few days after I was discharged. I was in no shape to travel and missed the event. The people in the group are very sensitive, kind, and powerful coaches. They were aware of my situation and followed it with interest. In fact, at the second meeting, they made a video expressing love and that they missed me. I got it after the event was over.

Between the second and third events, I wrote two books. *Meeting God at the Door*, and *The Book of Context*. Both books describe different parts of three encounters I had with God at the door between life and eternity.

The owner of the mastermind asked me to speak to the group. Both because of the extraordinary nature of the experience and because everyone was interested in knowing what happened.

I made a couple of notes and spoke for a little over an hour, barely pausing for breath. The experience was moving, and the power in the room was palpable.

Even feeling that myself, I was completely unprepared for the explosive ovation that spontaneously erupted at the end. I felt a little weak as I stood there and smiled and thanked the audience.

There were a few minutes for questions. I don't remember any of the questions except for the first one. A woman raised her hand and asked: "What is the biggest change that has manifest in your life since this experience?"

Not prepared for the question, I felt my mouth opening, and without hesitation, I said, "I no longer experience fear." I knew I had spoken truth, but I had no idea where the answer came from, except I knew it came straight from the center of the universe.

For the rest of the day, I talked to all those who had more questions and wanted a bit more detail about the experience. I brought copies of *Meeting God at the Door*, for everyone in the room.

I autographed several of them and expressed gratitude in each book for those who had shared care and concern for me during the ordeal.

For weeks I thought about how I answered that question and considered all the ways that it was true. This was in October, about three months after I left the hospital.

I had no idea what was coming five weeks later. More than I could have imagined was about to unfold. What was coming would strengthen my conviction and give me a framework to better explain the answer I gave.

"What if you knew…really knew
that you couldn't fail?"

Kellan Fluckiger

PART I
THE NATURE OF THE BEAST

When you have an experience like I did in the summer of 2018, it stands on its own in your mind. It is simultaneously so dramatic and traumatic that it seems impossible to be connected to a much larger flow of events.

After the near-death experience and the books I wrote, I expected to move forward with my coaching practice, armed with new insight, frameworks, and personal experience that would help me to serve more deeply and be a better catalyst for my present and future clients.

I also expected the experience to enhance my ability to create words and works of meaning, truth, and value. I knew for sure what my life mission was. It is to help every person understand and act on the four truths I learned in my conversations with God.

I believed I experienced the most powerful and profound transformation possible and was ready to move forward with the work I felt powerfully called to do.

You know the yearning. That feeling inside of you that makes you realize you have a purpose and mission. You may not know what it is, but you know you feel it, and you want to do something with it.

Physical rehabilitation was a tremendous struggle. I had a long way to go to get healthy. I assumed that work was all it needed – steady work on improving my physical condition and powerfully moving forward with my mission in the world.

How little we know. In the gentle, kind voice I have come to recognize, I can almost hear the divine presence speaking softly, "Not So… There is much more…"

With the benefit of hindsight, I now see the progression from the time I left the hospital to the next chapter in the astounding journey of life. As you read this, you will reflect on times in your life when things seem opaque at first and then, in retrospect, are crystal clear.

One glorious truth from this whole thing has been to experience the power of looking forward with crystal clarity that only comes from understanding that every event happens "for" us and not "to" us.

CHAPTER 1
THE TRUTH OF RECOVERY

One of the more dramatic effects of my MDD (Major Depressive Disorder) has been addictions of every shape and size. Consequently, I have decades of experience with the process of addiction and recovery.

In repeated efforts to overcome and get cleaned up, I have attended countless 12-step meetings and seen an endless parade of counselors. The truth is, recovery and healing is a gradual process.

Nothing about the growth of any kind is instantaneous. Plants don't grow that way, buildings don't get built that way, and the learning and growth in our lives doesn't happen overnight.

Understanding that truth is evident when you have that experience. I don't know why I thought that recovery from my month-long bout with a superbug (necrotizing MRSA) pneumonia in both lungs, two weeks in a coma, and losing 35 pounds in the process was going to be rapid.

But, like any growth process or addiction recovery, this rehab process was frustratingly slow.

When I left the hospital, I could barely walk, and I certainly couldn't do any exercise. For some reason, push-ups have been the measure of my fitness all my life, especially during the years I studied martial arts.

My greatest physical disappointment was trying to do push-ups after I got out of the hospital. I couldn't get my nose out of the carpet, not even once. I starkly realized how flatlined my body was; this was going to be a long process.

The truth of any recovery is that it is slow, and it takes work. Focus on the eventual goal, and dedicated constant rehearsal of tiny steps toward that goal are the daily fare on that journey.

I gradually realized that truth and settled in for the long haul. It seemed like a beautiful July that year. I don't remember much of it except wanting to spend a bit more of it outside.

Because I worked from home and sat in a chair to work, I started coaching clients once again and gradually returned to my regular coaching schedule — big gratitude for small things.

As the realities of my frailty and weakness slapped me in the face, my gratitude only increased. Seeing today the videos I made on Facebook at the time, I am shocked at the gaunt and haggard person in those clips.

CHAPTER 2
AUGUST

In retrospect, I understand that this whole experience was designed for growth. It was a wonderful opportunity and powerful learning that will shape my life forever. At the time, I was only experiencing torture.

When August came, I finally began some tiny amount of physical recovery. I was able to sit outside for periods of time, and pretty soon, I started walking.

The first time I went for a walk, I was grateful for the cane I got upon leaving the hospital. Walking was an ordeal that required heaving breaths at every step. Anyone walking by would have imagined I needed immediate medical attention.

The slowest walk caused me to huff and puff like I was in a race. Even with all that, I made it to the end of the block and back. I was excited.

The days went by slowly, and I made a little progress. My frustration level rose much faster than the physical recovery. I was beginning to be angry and hopeless at the same time.

I spent most of my life in fantastic physical condition. I earned a 2nd-degree black belt in a couple of martial arts. At age 40, I learned to ski – on double black diamond slopes, but none of that mattered.

I was blessed with a healthy body that bore up well despite all the abuse I heaped upon it during my years of addiction. I was angry that my prospects now looked like a life of limping and gasping for air.

Joy was invincible and the rock, just like she was during my stay in the hospital. She helped me calm down, helped me understand and accept that this pace was normal, and kept me sane.

Despite her best efforts, I often found myself teetering on the brink of despair. I would vacillate between hopeful excitement and bitter frustration.

I couldn't figure out why I had been given such gifts of knowledge and physically reduced to rubble. I guess part of the process of recovery was the journey of my mind through the minefield of brokenness.

For my body to heal to any degree, it was going to need a lot of time and attention. My mind was going to need similar work. Upon my leaving the hospital, the medical staff told me that it would take one to two years for my lungs to return to normal, if at all.

The damage and scarring in my lungs were considerable, and I wheezed in every conversation. As someone who makes their living speaking and who has a bunch of music to finish, I didn't know what was going to happen.

The days passed slowly, and my heart and emotions bounced all over the place. The doctors told me to expect symptoms of PTSD as a result of the coma and the trauma. I heard the words but didn't understand the meaning until it blasted me in the face in the coming weeks.

KELLAN FLUCKIGER

Chapter 3
Grieving – Denial, Anger, Bargaining

In the widely accepted model of grieving, the first three stages are Denial, Anger, and Bargaining. Fabulous books have been written about grieving, what each stage means and how each is beneficial in processing the events.

My denial was very complicated. My month in the hospital had physically destroyed me. I was withdrawn and angry. At the same time, I was extremely grateful for the experience I had with God at the door between life and eternity. It was difficult to reconcile the two competing feelings.

Because I had always been healthy and had a body I thought would serve me forever, being completely helpless was debilitating and frustrating.

Denial is helpful in the sense that it allows us to pace the grief we experience with a loss. By being in some degree of denial, we can cope with things a little at a time.

I couldn't deny I had been sick. I couldn't deny the conversations with God. What I got good at denying was the fact that it was going to be a long and complicated road to recovery.

In *Meeting God at the Door*, I described the miracle of my hospital release far earlier than expected. I wanted this physical thing to be handled just as fast – which wasn't going to happen.

As the days went by and the unrelenting reality of my shuffling gait and wheezing lungs became my new norm, the denial gradually subsided.

Anger is next, and for me, that was a familiar place. During my decades of depression, I was regularly angry to the point of rage, even without a particular reason. I was furious at my mother for the abuse she had heaped upon me. I was mad at how much of life I had either missed or ruined.

At the same time, I felt guilty because most of my adult life, I had failed to reject the false narrative that I was fundamentally flawed.

With that juxtaposition, my anger always turned inward and drove me to places of deeper depression, addictions, and attempted suicide – for decades. Anger was familiar and frightening. I didn't want to spend much time there.

The anger came and went in spurts as I battled with trying to get my body to cooperate and fearing that recovery would take forever. Deeper anger came from fear my lungs would never heal, and I wouldn't be able to sing and finish the albums I was working on.

This was confusing because I believed that the music and the books telling the story of my depression, addictions, and recovery were an essential part of my work. How could they be an essential part of my work if I'm blocked from completing them?

My anger came partly from the helplessness I felt and my perceived inability to make much difference in the process. The intensity of my desire to do the work I was called to do was off the charts, and in some ways, the anger strengthens that intensity.

Somewhere in my head, I knew my emotional state slowed my progress. The knowledge was intellectual and wasn't helping me much.

Like the denial, the anger gradually dissipated and began to manifest less and less in daily life. The more I understood, the more I could feel when it was coming and apply the techniques of meditation I learned over the years.

Bargaining is the third part, and for me, it was an interesting piece of this grieving process. I have always been an early riser. For some reason, I viewed getting up early as a sign of devotion and dedication. I also believed I would be rewarded with extraordinary accomplishments.

In one sense, it's true. If you get up early, you have more time to work on things than if you slept in. In another sense the bargaining was me hoping that if I kept a rigorous schedule, it would exponentially leverage the growth process.

Of course, it didn't work. When your body is broken, that logic is a double-edged sword. The less I slept and rested, the slower my physical recovery progressed. I was hoping for magic to offset the truth that my body needed weeks and months to accomplish the miracle of repair.

Like clockwork, the bargaining attitude of trying to trade something I could do for the truth of the healing process gradually left me. I allowed the physical and spiritual processes to take their course.

CHAPTER 4
GRIEVING – DEPRESSION AND ACCEPTANCE

Often in mourning a loss, the stages and the boundaries between them are fuzzy. I whipsawed back and forth between anger, bargaining, and depression many times.

The stage of depression got all tangled up with the depression that I struggled with all my life.

Sometimes I was convinced that this illness and the consequent trashing of my body was a punishment or just desserts for the life I've lived to this point.

My spiritual work told me this wasn't true, but there were many days when I felt like what was lost would be lost forever, and there was no way back.

Later I learned how true that was. There is absolutely no way back. Nothing will ever go back to the way it was. I will never have the experience of false invincibility I carried around like a "badge of honor." That is a good thing. That badge of honor led me to engage in careless and even reckless behavior. It caused much physical damage to my body.

Depression caused by a great loss is normal. It comes when you realize that no matter what happens, the person you lost or the situation you lost is gone forever. While a future situation may be wonderful and by some measure even better than whatever you lost, the loss is still real.

Even with an external illness as the true and obvious cause, my version of depression was full of "I'm not good enough" stories. The loss of my physical body, or what seemed like most of it, was simply proof that I had failed.

In my head, I knew that wasn't right, but the emotion was overwhelming. There were days when I was able to work on my body a lot. Other days, I had trouble if I walked too quickly up the two flights of stairs from the basement studios to the bedroom on the top floor.

Two things needed to happen to deal with the depression stage. First, I needed to disconnect what I was feeling about this situation from the lifetime of depression that said I was worthless and not good enough.

Mourning the loss of physical capability was necessary and important. It also needed to be mixed with the truth that gradually, things were getting better. It was only my worries that connected things to the old stories.

Taking the important step of disconnecting the decades-long story about my worth from the reality of the loss of help didn't happen all at once. It took love, attention, reassurance from Joy, and repeated work, but gradually it became clear there was a big difference.

The second part, the mourning of physical loss, was expected and normal. That was ok and must be allowed. Gradually I made my peace with that and realized I could and would move forward in returning myself to health. I would do all I could, but didn't know where the trail would go.

The final stage of grieving is acceptance. Of course, this doesn't mean pretending things never happened. It doesn't mean ignoring the consequences of the loss. It means acknowledging there is a future state with a new equilibrium.

Part of accepting that the future will be different from the past, meant I had to get comfortable with not knowing how well my body would respond, even over the long term. That was scary.

My doctors told me the lung damage was severe and may never heal. It was one thing to hear this prognosis and then bluster about how I would force my lungs to repair. It was quite another to make peace with the fact that I would do everything I could, and then see what happened.

I would work as hard as I could at a measured pace to get my body back in shape. I would regularly go to the doctor and see what could be done for my lungs.

I chose to understand that everything happens "for" me instead of "to" me. This is a staple of personal development literature and philosophy. It's one thing to know that and quite another to accept it in a difficult circumstance.

I worked to create that acceptance as the days went by. No surprise that some days are better than others. Gradually the determination spoke louder than the resignation. By the end of August, I was at about 50%.

CHAPTER 5
SEPTEMBER – EXCITEMENT, PUSH-UPS, AND PREPARATION

September started. Summer was winding down though I missed most of it. The weather was beautiful. I increased my walking distance to ½ a mile or so. After every walk, I needed a good rest.

Still using push-ups as a measure for progress, I kept track of how the numbers went up. Still, I had a weird relationship with push-ups. Some days I wanted to see what I could do, and other days I felt reluctant because I worried I would backslide.

My excitement came from three different places. First, the number of push-ups I could do was increasing, the length of my walks was gradually getting longer, and that meant physical things were looking up.

Second, I began attending my BNI networking group after a 3-month absence. Being "back in action," felt like something even though it was small. At least I wasn't housebound or completely wiped out after a trip out.

Third, I had accepted and was planning to attend four speaking opportunities in October. I hadn't planned for October to be so busy, it just lined up – every weekend was a multi-day event where I was scheduled to be on stage.

I'm not sure it was a good idea, but I was determined to see it through; plus, it was exciting. It marked the beginning of a real return to business. My focus turned to preparation for the events.

The first was a 3-day video summit. This was the fifth year of its existence, and I had been the MC every year. I wanted to continue. It also provided the opportunity to meet some movers and shakers in the YouTube world, which was exciting.

The second was the final mastermind I referred to in the prologue. I was excited about that one because of how kind everyone was when I missed the July event and because I had been asked to speak about my experience and the books I was finishing.

The third was in Philadelphia. I would have the room for seven hours. *The Book of Context* would be done, and I was stoked to have a place to talk about what had happened so soon after my hospital ordeal.

The last was in Phoenix and bridged the end of October and November. This event was put on by a client, and I was part of the faculty. I knew I would meet many new people and provide help to my client. These four events would be the first reprieve Joy had in many months.

I don't know if it was a good idea to have that busy of a schedule so soon after the serious event, but that's what I had accepted and was determined to do. I think part of the excitement came because I had been basically out of commission for several months. It was time to get moving.

As the month went on, my push-up count went up, my preparations were going ok and I was starting to feel much better. Finally, the day before starting the road trip, probably in a rush of adrenaline, I broke a new barrier on the push-up front. I had just done 45 of the beasties. I knew that I was well on the way to recovery.

I still coughed a lot and got winded after five minutes of aerobic exercise, but I was in far better shape and higher spirits than where I started. Things were looking up.

KELLAN FLUCKIGER

CHAPTER 6
OCTOBER 9 – NOVEMBER 4

Now that we were underway, the reality of performance kicked in. Being out of commission for four months was intimidating. I didn't know how I would feel as the month wore on, or how I would do at each of the venues. I was determined to go all-in but did not know how my body would react. I had a habit of biting off big chunks and then going like mad to make it fit.

My desired outcome for the month was to do a great job for the event owners, meet some people, have some fun, and perhaps get some prospects for future business opportunities.

At the first event in Los Angeles, Joy and I had a great time. We did some touristy stuff, drove through Beverly Hills, and went to several shopping centers of renown. Thankfully, Joy is great at putting together an awesome itinerary, which I rely completely on her for, as I haven't ever been much of a tourist.

The event went well, and I did good as the MC. As a bonus, I had the opportunity to meet some big names in the YouTube world and got some great storytelling ideas. I was amazed by some of the stories of grit and determination that

I heard from speakers who had their own tough times. This all fits right in with *The Book of Context*.

The second event was in Scottsdale, AZ. It was amazing. The learning was good; the people were precious and warmly welcomed me "back from the dead." Also, sincere ovation and insightful questions were experiences to be savored.

On top of that, one person got an 11" x 17" card that said, "It's just possible that you have no idea how much is possible." Everyone signed it with kind thoughts and well-wishes. It was both a surprise and a precious moment of inspiration. It will hang forever on my wall.

The third event in Philadelphia went well. I spoke for 7 hours total and was deeply grateful for the opportunity and the support of those who came. I told the story of what happened in the hospital and of my conversations with God at the door between life and eternity.

I also taught from *The Book of Context*, the first book in this series. All these opportunities to rehearse what had happened and to answer questions about what I saw, felt, and learned were amazing additions to the growing certainty that I needed to write more about this powerful truth.

The last event in Phoenix felt different. It went well, and I spoke four times over the three days of the event. I was there mostly to support my client as he delivered his event. Three of the talks were short and topic-specific to my client's curriculum.

The fourth was much longer. There was no agenda. I talked about the challenges of being human and doing new and sometimes difficult things. I told some of the story, but mostly concentrated on the truth that we have complete control of our destiny if we choose to take it.

It resonated deeply and differently than the event in Scottsdale. There was a deeply spiritual and motivating context to the time we spent together. Though I hadn't intended it as a "book sales" event, many bought books until I ran out. More importantly, I cherished the chance to write words of encouragement and love for each person who bought one.

The feeling made me reflect again and again on how much we have been given, how big our opportunities are, and how we truly are at our best when we are serving each other.

It inspired me to write the outline of the next book I planned to write: *The Results Equation*. We got home, tired, but spiritually refreshed. More than ever I was committed to the purpose and mission I had been given during my conversations with God.

CHAPTER 7
NOVEMBER STASIS AND THE SLIPPERY SLOPE

We didn't have anything planned for the rest of the year except normal coaching business from home and local events. I was also finishing up working on some videos for a marketing campaign and I continued to go to my BNI chapter.

Winter was coming early. This made it harder to exercise, and I stayed indoors more. Then I got frustrated with myself and tried to push physical recovery too hard.

Something was changing, and I didn't know what it was. I got more tired when I walked instead of feeling better and blamed it on the weather. I found myself sleeping more. Something was not ok and I knew it.

According to the doctors, none of this was unusual, but I wanted it NOT to happen. Joy was tireless in trying to get me to "let it be" and take things in stride. I was not having any of it.

Somewhere around mid-November, I decided to take a walk in the ravine that's near our house.

It is a beautiful place and has great walking and biking trails. I have walked there hundreds of times.

The snow had already begun to collect, and we were in the middle of an extended freeze where daytime highs were below freezing. This meant that the sidewalks and streets had permanent snow and ice.

I went where I normally enter the ravine, and the trail downward was icy and slick. I was careful as I went, but halfway down the trail I slipped and fell. It was not a serious fall and I didn't think much of it.

I completed my walk and came home and felt proud of myself for the effort. The next day I was a little stiff, undoubtedly because I fell.

My mood was bad. I was trying to understand why things were going backward. After a couple of days, my back started to hurt up behind the left scapula.

Nothing serious, but it was painful enough that the only way I could sleep was lying in a certain position. I took more pain meds and ignored it.

The Saturday after U.S. Thanksgiving, I exercised harder than normal. Besides the morning routine stretching, push-ups, and leg exercises, I went for an extended 3-mile walk.

All during the walk, the left side of my upper back was in throbbing pain. My frustration was throbbing right along with it. I kept going and believed if I stretched out afterward, all would be okay.

During the last few days of November, my condition worsened. Sleep was difficult and finding the right position with my left shoulder propped up a particular way was getting nearly impossible. If I sat for very long, I was in pain. When I stood up, it was difficult to stand up straight. I didn't know what was going on or what to do.

I started to get scared.

KELLAN FLUCKIGER

Chapter 8
December 1 – 5

When December started, each day stretched into an eternity, which is a complete story unto itself. On Saturday, December 1, I realized it wasn't going away, so I tried to "figure out" what *exactly* happened to bring so much back pain.

I remembered the fall in the ravine a couple of weeks earlier. That wasn't enough to be the whole problem. Then I remembered the previous Saturday where I pushed so hard in exercising and decided I must've done some damage. Underneath it all was something nagging.

On Sunday, December 2, I went to church, but with great difficulty. I play the organ in the service every Sunday and I wanted to do what I was supposed to. Also, I was hoping the focus on worship and music would help.

I made it through the worship service and had to leave immediately. I couldn't stay for Sunday School class because I was in too much pain. I came home and tried to sleep in the afternoon. With just a little dozing here and there, the day finally ended.

On Monday, December 3, I had no scheduled appointments outside the home. I had five coaching calls of one hour each. Completing all those calls was an ordeal by itself, but I took breaks and made it through the day.

I was trying to figure out if I had "hit bottom" yet and whether this was going to start getting better or if this was the beginning of something much worse. I really couldn't tell. It got worse.

On Tuesday, December 4, I was supposed to get up early and go to our weekly 7:00 am BNI meeting. I got up to go and was in such pain that it wasn't happening. In this networking group, you commit to attend every week or send a substitute.

I had made no arrangements, so I woke Joy up and asked if she wanted to sub for me. She said yes, and I went back to bed. I couldn't sleep and tossed restlessly until I got up at 8:30 a.m.

I had six hours of scheduled coaching calls – that was going to be difficult. I decided to do them anyway and focused on the work at hand. Tuesday night, I didn't go with Joy to the weekly 12-step meeting we facilitate through our church. This 12-step group that we facilitate is important to me because of my experience with addictions. I love the opportunity to help those who are struggling.

I realized that something was wrong and getting worse, but I wasn't sure what to do next.

The morning of Wednesday, December 5, answered all questions. I had coaching calls scheduled starting at 7:30 a.m., so I had to get up at least by seven to be on time.

My phone alarm sounded, and I reached over and grabbed at it to stop the noise before it woke up Joy. I rolled slowly over to get out of bed and go downstairs to start my calls.

I moved my left leg to put it on the floor and stand up, and it suddenly began behaving like it had a mind of its own. It twitched and jerked and would not settle down – I had no control of my leg. Using my hand, I pulled my right leg over to see if this would help, and it behaved the same way. I tried to stand up and collapsed to the floor. My face was on the carpet, and I couldn't feel my legs. Not comprehending what was happening, I tried to get up on my hands and knees to crawl to the bathroom and collapsed again on my face.

It dawned on me that this was serious. The only possible direction of motion for me was *down*. I realized I had no control over anything below my waist. I lay there on the floor, face down, trying to figure out what to do next.

CHAPTER 9
THE SHOCK SETS IN

After a few minutes of face down in the carpet; I went through different possible scenarios in my mind. I realized I had no idea what was going on. Still, in denial, all the situations I entertained were focused on how I could somehow manage to get to the bathroom and then to my desk to do my work for the day.

I refused to consider the obvious. This was an emergency and required urgent attention. It's funny what we can see later that is as opaque as obsidian at the moment.

I crawled on my arms to the bathroom and pulled myself up to use the facilities. My upper back was in terrible pain, and I had no feeling or control below the waist. I called out to Joy because I knew I couldn't do any more by myself. I told her what was going on, and she wanted to call 911 immediately.

Stupidly, I resisted and still wanted to see if I could get downstairs to my desk. I somehow believed that if I could get seated upright in my chair, I could complete the hours of coaching I had between 8:00 a.m. and 2:00 p.m.

Using my arms, I wormed to the top of the stairs and stopped, perplexed. We have dog gates at the bottom of the stairs up to the bedrooms. We also have a gate at the top of the stairs leading to the basement. I'd have to navigate both to get to my desk.

With Joy's help, I turned around and went down the stairs on my backside with my useless legs dangling in front of me. At the bottom of the staircase, we lifted my legs through the narrow opening of the dog gate, and I tried to hoist my torso through the narrow opening using my arms.

I failed and knocked the gate out of its place. It crashed to the floor, and I sat panting, trying to figure out what to do next.

I was still determined to make it downstairs to my desk. Joy watched helplessly as I muscled my way over to the staircase to go to my office in the basement.

A second dog gate stood in the way. It might as well have been a thousand-foot steel barrier. This dog gate is fastened much more securely, so there would be no knocking it down like I had the first gate.

We struggled mightily for 10 minutes or so trying to navigate the narrow opening. It became clear that this was not going to happen.

Finally, it dawned on me that I wasn't going to ignore this. I couldn't pretend it wasn't happening. I could not power my way through and hope it got better. This was serious.

Now I had a whole new set of problems. I was helpless and broken. Five people were waiting, each in their turn, to have a call with me – their coach. I couldn't fulfill this responsibility.

The only thing I was focused on was that failure. The truth of the severity of my situation had not fully penetrated my consciousness.

CHAPTER 10
PANIC

After we rested a few minutes, I wanted to crawl across the living room floor and somehow get up on the couch so we could talk about what to do next. A growing sense of worry bordering on panic was beginning to choke me.

I made it across the living room floor, and somehow, we got my body up onto the couch. I lay there panting, and we made a plan to handle the clients.

I asked Joy to call everyone or send them a message and cancel the coaching calls for the day. Normally I reschedule when some urgent thing happens, but I realized I didn't know what was going on and couldn't say anything with certainty.

I lay there as she made those arrangements. After she finished canceling appointments and explaining what we didn't know, she came back, and we talked about what to do next.

The pain in my back was intense, I had no sensation or ability to move anything below the waist, and I began to wonder in the most profound way what was going on. Fear was peering at me like a monster.

We talked about what happened just six months earlier. The near-death experience and the visits with God at the door between life and eternity. The commitments and plans I made.

We talked about the two books I wrote from that experience. We talked about the speaking engagements we did in October and how good we felt about what we had done.

I didn't understand what was going on in my body. I thought my trial was done; I was getting busy doing my work in the world. My mind was reeling as I finally started to contemplate what must've been obvious for some time. This was serious, and I was broken again.

We finally concluded that we had to call the paramedics and go to the hospital. It was more like I came to that conclusion. She had been there from the first moment I collapsed upstairs.

Joy called 911, and I lay there waiting for the ambulance. I have never gone to the hospital in an ambulance. I had no idea what to expect.

The pain was bad enough that I was struggling with consciousness. I think I dozed off for a few minutes because the next thing I knew, there were people in the room, and they were talking to me.

I described the ordeal of the morning to the paramedics and explained that I had no sensation below the waist and no ability to move my legs.

They asked a few more questions and then concluded we were making an immediate trip to the ER. They manipulated me so that they could hoist me up onto the stretcher. There were three of them, so it wasn't too hard.

They were well-trained and smoothly got me onto the stretcher. A wild parade of thoughts flashed through my mind. I remembered countless scenes of ambulances and rescues and emergencies from movies and television. I had never observed such a scene from the horizontal position.

The ambulance looks different from the stretcher. They hoisted me inside and closed the door. I was left there alone with my thoughts as they finished preparations to go to the hospital. Joy was going to follow in the car.

At this moment, reality began to sink in. I was in an ambulance on my way to the emergency room, paralyzed from the waist down and in severe back pain. What was going on?

KELLAN FLUCKIGER

CHAPTER 11
BACK TO THE BRINK

We live about 15 or 20 minutes from the hospital depending on traffic. It was early afternoon so I expected the emergency vehicle to get there in 15 minutes.

As the reality of my situation settled deeper and deeper, I began to think about what all this meant. I had the powerful certainty that there was a connection between this situation and what happened during the summer. I began to contemplate where this might go and what to do next.

When I realized with complete certainty that there was a connection, and this was an ongoing part of the whole growth experience provided by the conversations with God in the summer, then, despite the pain, my mind shifted to one single question.

"What is the gift in this experience?" I repeated that question over and over and brought my mind to think about the benefits, blessings, and learnings that already were and would continue to come to me because of this new twist in the road.

I began to list the blessings. I realized this taught me humility. I realized this was an opportunity to appreciate life more. I wondered what things I had missed from the conversations with God six months earlier.

As I sat in meditation on this train of thought, the pain in my back came into focus. I asked myself, "What is this trying to teach me?" Suddenly a picture appeared in my mind. I guess you could call it a vision.

Occasionally, I have seen bits of poker tournaments on television. I'm not a fan, but tournaments come on after some sporting events Joy and I watch. Always in casinos, and they always look about the same. I could see the people seated around the table with piles of chips in front of them.

I saw the scene through my own eyes as a participant, seated at the table. Everyone else at the table faded away, and directly across from me was the Grim Reaper. I couldn't see his face, just the familiar black hood and the blackness where the face should be.

He reached down and pushed a massive pile of chips into the center of the table. I don't know what cards I held, and it didn't matter. It got cold and suddenly, this thought ran through my mind.

"When you play poker, and your adversary raises the bet, you have two choices. You either Fold or Call." I lay there focused on the vision. I realized it was my turn to react and that the decision before me was massive but simple.

With tears streaming down my face and the crescendo of agony in my back, reaching a peak, I repeated the words to myself, "You either Fold or Call."

I imagined a picture of throwing down my cards and giving up. A sick sensation swept over me, and I knew that would not be me, not now, not ever.

With all the strength I could muster, I slammed my right arm to the stretcher and through gritted teeth, with the most powerful voice I could use, I half croaked; half-shouted, "Then I Call."

With the decision fiercely pronounced, the vision slowly faded. Just a few minutes later, we arrived at the emergency room of the University of Alberta hospital.

The flurry of activity getting out of the ambulance and into the emergency room was all background noise. I could think about nothing else except the singularity of the scene that had just played out in my mind.

I repeated to myself over and over again, "Then I Call."

CHAPTER 12
THE EMERGENCY ROOM

Every other time I've been to the emergency room, I came in under my own power. That meant I sat in a chair, waited until the triage nurse called me and asked me what was wrong. The nurse listens to the story and then decides how urgent your case is.

When that happens, your waiting is punctuated by emergency people brought in by paramedics on stretchers. This was the first time I was one of "those" people.

They wheeled me right up to the admission nurse and told them what was going on. There was no question about being admitted to the hospital, and everything happened in a few minutes.

I was wheeled into one of the curtained-off areas to wait for the next available medical staff member to begin the intake process.

I really don't know how long I lay there. The pain was bad, and my mind went in and out of coherence. The sounds of the emergency room were all around me and I lay there waiting.

After a bit, Joy came in and waited with me. Eventually, a nurse came in and asked me all the normal questions. The interruption pulled me back to reality, and I described what happened that morning and the two weeks prior.

They looked at my medical history and saw the records from six months earlier. That prompted immediate isolation. The superbug routine means everyone in the room was gowned, gloved, and masked at all times.

They gave me IV pain medication to lower the volume in my head, and we waited. A couple of doctors came in sequence, and I repeated the story.

There were many questions about the events of the summer. They were particularly interested in the follow-up that happened. There wasn't any follow-up after my discharge in July, so I had nothing to say.

They acted surprised, and I wasn't sure if I should be worried about that. It didn't matter now. Eventually, the doctors ordered an MRI to see what was going on in my upper back.

They wheeled me out of the emergency room to the place in the hospital where they did MRI scans. When I got there, they ask standard questions in preparation for that test. One of the questions was about earlier surgeries.

Did I have any implants or devices in my body? Yes. About ten years earlier, I had an operation called a laser stapedotomy in both of my ears. This procedure drilled a hole in the anvil and put a device there to help with hearing.

I had fairly severe hearing loss at the time and had been wearing hearing aids for several years. This operation had restored 70% of my hearing. That meant for the last ten years, I no longer needed to wear hearing aids.

That was all well and good except they told me I couldn't have an MRI unless I could find proof that the implants, small as they were, were MRI safe. I remembered receiving a card that said that the devices were MRI tolerant.

My assurances were not adequate, so they wouldn't do the procedure. Joy went to try to find the card. I had absolutely no hope that she could find it. I had no idea where it was and hadn't seen it for years. In addition, we moved from Phoenix to Alberta 21 months earlier.

As part of the de-junking for the move, we gave away 500 boxes full of "stuff." Yes, 500. You know what happens when you live in a big house for years. You accumulate an endless amount of nothing.

I lay hopelessly on a stretcher in the hallway, waiting for a couple of hours. To my complete amazement and as an incredible blessing, Joy presented the card to the hospital staff – she found the card.

I had carried it in my wallet for years but stopped for some reason. I have no idea how she found it except to say that she was divinely guided where to look.

Even with medication, the pain in my back was intense. I was not at all certain that I could lay still for 45 minutes while they did the MRI.

Fortunately, my decades of meditation practice plus the medication allowed me to focus and relax enough to get the MRI completed. After all this drama, it was about 9:00 p.m.

CHAPTER 13
THE SURGERY

The spinal surgeon on call was sent the results of my MRI. He was finishing a surgery at a hospital a few miles away. I waited for the results of his evaluation still lying on the stretcher outside of the MRI chamber.

As time passed, Joy relayed comments from the medical staff about the spinal surgeon on call. He was the best in the business. They said we were "really lucky" that this was his night. I don't believe in luck. There are no accidents, and I knew it was a blessing.

After a while, the report came in. The surgeon had ordered us to proceed immediately to the Operating Room. He said I needed emergency spinal surgery, right now, in the middle of the night. The review of the MRI convinced him it was urgent.

I went straight from the ER to the OR without ever being admitted to the hospital. The whole situation was taking on epic proportions.

I had been asking since we left the house in the ambulance to recognize the blessings in this situation. The miracles were mounting thick and fast. I had the vision in the ambulance. Next, came the miracle of finding the MRI card for my hearing devices. Now we were having emergency midnight surgery. This whole thing was off the charts.

I saw the doctor for a few minutes before we went into surgery. He introduced himself and told me that the MRI revealed a sizable abscess in my spinal column. From what he could see, the infection was at least four inches long with calcification at the bottom. There was considerable pus in the abscess, and the situation required immediate attention.

The infection was located between the C-2 and the T-1 vertebrae. That is at the top of the neck and represented a significant threat to life. His opinion was that the infection had been growing for several weeks and that the abscess had begun to harden and put pressure on the spine.

That was the explanation for my loss of mobility. He said if we didn't operate right away, I could die or become permanently paralyzed because the infection was so high up in the neck.

Joy asked how long the surgery would be. The doctor was vague and said he wouldn't know until he got inside to see what was going on.

He asked more questions about my previous lung infection and anything unusual that happened since July. He was trying to decide if this was a recurrence of the MRSA bacteria that had nearly killed me a few months earlier.

He asked if I had questions. I didn't have the presence of mind to ask anything. I was still reeling from the fact that this had all happened and that suddenly I was going to have emergency spinal surgery.

He introduced me to the anesthesiologist. It turns out that this doctor was also another heavyweight who just "happened" to be on call. He told me he would see me on the "other side." We went into the operating room. They put a mask on me and told me to breathe deeply. I don't remember anything else until I woke up a couple of hours later, the operation completed.

CHAPTER 14
INTENSIVE CARE

The next thing I remember, we were outside the operating room, and I came out of the anesthetic. The doctor told us that the operation had been successful. They drained over 10 mL of pus from the abscess.

They also performed a laminectomy. This is a procedure where they scrape the inside of the spinal vertebrae to create more room for the spinal cord. The infection had hardened and shrunk the size of the channel.

It had been pressing on the spinal cord near the T-1 or the T-2 vertebrae, which was causing all the pain and loss of mobility. It occurred to me at the time that the tiniest movement in error could have damaged or severed the spinal cord. The best outcome of that situation would be permanent paralysis. The worst outcome was death.

He told me I was "lucky" that I came in when I did. He told me I was "lucky" that it wasn't much worse. He told me I was "lucky" that everything in the surgery had gone as well as it had. I knew that luck had nothing to do with it, and I was grateful beyond words.

I was overwhelmed with gratitude. We had been blessed with a skilled surgeon at the top of his game. He also told us that it was unusual to have that type of infection actually inside the spinal column. The spinal fluid operates in a sterile environment. Somehow the bacteria had come into that space and created the disaster.

They took a bacteria sample to test for MRSA. Because of the previous risk, I was kept in isolation. It was now sometime after 1:00 a.m. on the morning of December 6. They were trying to find me a room in the ICU.

I was on supplemental oxygen because of low saturation levels. The high level of supplemental oxygen I was receiving meant that no one in a standard ward would take me. I had to stay in the Intensive Care Unit – the ICU again, aka "old home week."

Between the lingering effects of the anesthetic and the pain medication, I was finally able to get a bit of sleep. I had to be careful about how I lay in the bed and any movement because the pain was just a fractional movement away.

Though partially sedated, the pain was intense enough that the thought of having full consciousness and no painkillers were terrifying.

I stayed in the ICU for most of the day on December 7. Late in the afternoon, the oxygen level required was reduced enough to move me to one of the recovery wards.

Everywhere I went, because of the "isolation," everyone had to don the now-familiar yellow gowns with masks and gloves every time they came into my room.

Finally, the frantic level of activity that accompanied the last two days slowed. I was able to think more deeply and clearly about what was going on. I began again to list the blessings of this event.

For some reason, my mind reflected on the answer I gave weeks earlier when someone asked me, "What is the biggest change in your life since your visit with God?" My answer was, "I no longer feel fear."

I said that in October and now just five weeks later, I was again staring death in the face. I was blessed with miraculous timing getting to the hospital. I was blessed with the vision and the choice to go all in.

I was blessed with a talented surgeon. I was blessed again with the astounding support of an amazing wife and life partner.

Waves of gratitude swept over me. Not focused on the fact that my life had been spared again, but rather on the tangible yet spiritual nature of this whole experience and the very thin veil between this life and the next.

I realized deeply and completely that I was not afraid. I knew this would pass. I knew this was part of a process of refinement and growth. I knew it affirmed what I learned in the summer.

Each of us is a divine being. Each of us has assignments we eagerly agreed to do while we were here. Each of us has gifts and talents needed to complete those assignments. Each of us has access to all the help we need to complete our mission and live in joyous fulfillment and happiness – no matter what happens along the way.

Our sacred choice is whether we will seek and find these opportunities and fulfill them or choose some other path. Settle for the obvious or strive for the glorious. Fold or Call.

My assignment is to figure out how to connect everything and make it useful to everyone I work with now and in the future.

CHAPTER 15
METAMORPHOSIS

Much like a caterpillar turning into a butterfly, the next few days in the hospital were a period of metamorphosis. So much came into my mind in the hours I had to lay and ponder the meaning and value of this experience.

Sometime in the next day or two, the doctor told me my blood tested positive for MRSA. I was infected again, and once again, it had wreaked havoc in my system.

Considering what happened six months earlier and the fact that this was the second occurrence, the doctors were planning a more aggressive outpatient treatment strategy following my eventual discharge.

The first night after the surgery, the pain was so intense that I did not sleep. The next morning (December 7), I told the doctor I needed medication because I wasn't sleeping at all.

They upped the pain medication and put me on a regular dosage every three hours so that I could relax and sleep. That worked. I was able to start a path to recovery.

I had a neck brace to hold my neck in a certain position. This was to allow the healing to take place more effectively. Over the weekend, the routine of regular nurse visits and vital signs and pain medication kicked in. I settled in for the rhythm of recovery.

Every morning the infectious disease specialist came in and told me I still tested positive for MRSA. They had me on high dose specialty antibiotics to get that cleared. Finally, on December 9, we got the first negative result. It was working.

Monday, December 10, was my 63rd birthday. It was an interesting experience to have my birthday so soon after this life-threatening situation. Getting older causes us to think about our mortality. My recent brush with death gave me a renewed appreciation and determination for life.

For some reason, they never found the blood test taken on my birthday, December 10. So that day didn't count. To consider release from the hospital, they needed three days of negative tests in a row.

The first negative test was on December 9, December 10 didn't count because they lost it. They needed a negative test on December 11 and December 12 before we could begin discussing plans for discharge.

I started a ramp down with the painkillers because the last thing in the world I needed was another possible source of chemical madness in my life permanently.

On Tuesday, December 11, the test was also negative. I was canceling all of my client calls one day at a time because I was too weak to talk to anyone.

I made several videos that I posted to Facebook from my hospital bed. I didn't do this for sympathy; I did it because of the deep discoveries I was experiencing about the role that fear, adversity and choice play in all our lives.

It was becoming clearer and clearer to me that we have the divine right to choose so many things about our lives. We often ignore that and let things just happen. If we choose to exercise it, we can create anything we wish.

On December 12, I conducted all my coaching calls, neck brace, and all, propped up in a chair in my hospital room. All my clients graciously agreed to postpone, but I wanted to take advantage of the opportunity to share what I had learned to the extent I thought it might matter in the challenges they were facing.

The sessions I had that day were powerful and meaningful both for the clients and for me. It is so interesting what a change in perspective can do if we are open.

Expecting a negative test for the 12th, I began asking about possible release dates. The 12th test came back negative. Even so, they told me that the earliest possible release date would be Monday the 17th, and that was doubtful. I told them I had something scheduled for Saturday the 15th and I wanted to go home Friday afternoon, December 14th.

One doctor among all of them listened. He understood what I was trying to accomplish. He took it upon himself to personally see what he could do to get the tests completed, the paperwork done, and the necessary permission lined up so that I could go home Friday afternoon.

His diligence and personal choice to help me made the difference. All the necessary arrangements were made so that I could be discharged on Friday afternoon. The only reason that happened is because of his personal dedication and commitment.

Once again, I saw demonstrated the power of individual resolve. Regardless of the number of people in opposition, regardless of the circumstances, a single individual with resolve makes things happen.

Part of the drama of arranging the aftercare was that I would be on intravenous antibiotics for six weeks after my discharge. That meant I needed to get a PICC line inserted into my upper right arm.

I never heard of such a thing. It is a "Peripheral Inserted Central Catheter." It's inserted underneath the upper right arm and goes all the way across the chest inside the veins and empties right into the heart.

The follow-up antibiotics were so strong the only place they could be administered was directly into the heart. If they were infused in a vein in the arm, the antibiotics would collapse the vein in very short order.

I needed to have these antibiotics for six weeks. That meant I would be carrying around a bag with a pump as a companion for forty-two days after I got out.

Part of the work that my champion doctor had to do was arrange the procedure to insert the PICC line. That department was booked. It got scheduled. Then we had to get the home care arranged. Twice a week, someone needed to come and change the line and inspect the pump. Somehow that all got arranged.

Going home this time was completely different from my discharge in July. In the summer, I was discharged and left on my own. Given the recurrence, I was put on a rigorous weekly blood testing schedule, homecare schedule and antibiotic regime.

We were all determined to have no more recurrences of the monster. I was grateful for all the attention and focus given to this situation.

I was also grateful to the doctor who championed my cause for release on the day I created in my mind.

More than anything, this entire drama demonstrated to me the truth of the principles I wrote in the books *Meeting God at the Door*, and *The Book of Context*. The two books I wrote after the near-death experience last summer.

For reasons only known to the divine, this additional experience with all its complexity and beauty was a capstone to the whole series.

Just as I created in my mind, all the necessary parts fell into place, and one by one, the dissenting doctors all agreed to discharge me on Friday afternoon, December 14. It was once again a small sign of the power of declaration, determination and the ability each of us has to create our lives.

I left the hospital overflowing with gratitude and certainty about the path ahead. I had no idea how long recovery would take or where the path would lead. What I knew for sure was that I had been blessed once again with protection and opportunity.

I felt once again deeply committed to the purpose and mission I have in life. That mission is to help every single person understand their divinity and discover, develop, and manifest their divine gifts.

It is the reason I draw breath.

The event I scheduled on Saturday went off without a hitch. Once again, I found myself home, weak but fiercely determined to walk the path I had seen.

I knew that a great deal of work lay ahead. I also knew I had no idea exactly how to proceed. Furthermore, I knew that if I started moving, things would become clear, the path would manifest, and the journey would be amazing.

"True freedom comes from letting go of the need to control."

Kellan Fluckiger

PART II
FRAMEWORK FOR FREEDOM

The next four weeks provided an amazing space to create the framework for *Walking Without Fear*. A framework is a structure that describes a set of principles, how they fit together, and what they accomplish. Frameworks are designed to be memorable and powerful to effectively convey the truths they teach.

There are no accidents. My discharge from the hospital just coming up to the holiday season was the perfect opportunity to meditate, consolidate, and formulate the things I had learned.

Not just what I learned from this incredible experience with the abscess in my back and facing death once again. Far more than that. The consolidation started with everything I learned during and after the conversations with God in June up to and including the present day.

Just a few of the most recent parts of this path include:

- The timing of the recurrence of MRSA,
- The availability of the capable surgeon that would opt for emergency surgery,

- Choosing to return to coaching while still in the hospital and very weak,
- Creating a discharge date so I could keep my scheduled commitments,
- Having a block of time to myself to both heal and create.

More than anything, the arrangement of events provided time and space needed to receive the rest of the inspiration and knowledge I want so badly to give you.

When I answered the question in October and said, "I no longer experience fear," I spoke the truth. I didn't yet realize the full meaning of what I said. That was to come during this later period.

Imagine for a moment living even one day completely unconstrained by fear or worry. Imagine living in the complete certainty that there is always a way forward and that every experience in your life can be turned for your benefit.

We hear such expressions often and sometimes dismiss it as the ravings of lunatics or fanatics who are looking for divine explanations for everything.

My experiences, both the miraculous and the mundane, have helped me know with absolute certainty that life, God, and the universe are conspiring for our good and growth.

This section will describe the framework for living your life without fear. How you choose to use it will determine how effective it is for you.

Fear is a creation of the mind and the most debilitating barrier to the accomplishment of our divine potential. Other than immediate physical danger, fear is primarily a useless construct that keeps us from realizing great opportunities and growth.

If you slow down and think about a day-to-day experience, you'll realize that fear is part of your everyday decision-making process.

Fear and believing the worst about the future is the driver that keeps us from growth, experimenting with new ideas, and stretching to create what is possible.

One way this shows up is thinking of all the reasons why something before us is a bad idea or won't work, even when we feel like something is good.

What if you knew you couldn't fail? What if you knew there was a pot of gold at the end of the rainbow? Would anything stop you from going to find it?

What beliefs have we internalized so deeply that we give up easily and settle for so little when the opportunity is infinite?

Change and growth is the real story of life. Time and choice are the substance from which life is made. As I share with you what I learned and what I know to be real, consider how this power can liberate you and bless everyone in your life.

CHAPTER 16
KNOWING AND NOT KNOWING

One great fear is the fog created by "not knowing." The unknown, the uncertain, the tentative are all situations where fear clouds our thinking, shrinks possibilities and camouflages opportunities. Especially when the stakes are high, or we have a story that the stakes are high.

The funny thing about this is even when we think we know, we still don't know. We might believe something is going to happen, and it turns out completely different.

So, in the midst of knowing we still don't know. Somehow the belief that we know creates comfort and pushes fear into the background or eliminates it.

In creating a life without fear, it's more useful to think about this as "believing vs. not believing." When we have a belief only in a negative outcome, we feel helpless and sometimes hopeless. That translates to the sick feeling in the stomach that is often a flag of fear.

The future, even one second from now, is uncertain. We think we know what is coming based on what has happened before or what is happening right now. Reality is anything can happen at any time and often does.

Not knowing and the fear it generates is mostly grounded in the sense of "no control." When we know what is going to happen, it seems like everything is in its place. Even if it's not our doing, knowing what is coming feels like control.

I didn't know what was going to happen when I went to the hospital. I didn't know what was going to happen when I went in for an operation. I didn't know if I would live through the experience.

When I came out alive and woke up, I didn't know how long recovery would take. I didn't know what had caused the problem in the first place. I didn't know if the operation would completely solve the problem or if this was just a Band-Aid.

There were more things I didn't know than I did know. As all this passed through my mind, I realized the choice I made in the ambulance, to "call" no matter what happened, was decisive.

I didn't need to know. My choice was to move forward from one second to the next, without having any idea what the world one minute from now might look like.

The key is becoming comfortable with not knowing. You don't control the actions, attitudes, or thoughts of anyone around you. You don't control the weather, society, elections, or the economy. In fact, you don't control much at all. The *only* thing you control is your attitude and the actions you take in any situation.

Combining the fact that we control almost nothing with the helplessness that comes from the sense of "no control," we end up living in a state of perpetual frustration, anger, and fear. If you become comfortable with not knowing and realize that all you ever control is your own attitude, actions, and thoughts, then there is nothing to worry about.

What does it mean to become comfortable with not knowing? Does that mean we shouldn't make any plans at all? Should we have no belief or expectation that any plans we make will come to fruition? Of course not. We make plans, and we will continue to make them. We continue to work on things we plan as hard as we can.

What I learned was that contentment comes from a choice to do the best I can in each minute of life, without making assumptions or "needing to know" what the outcome one minute, one hour, one day, one week, or one year from today might be.

For me, the first step in learning to walk through the world without fear was to choose to be okay with not knowing.

How does that happen?

What does it mean to know in the first place?

<u>Coming to Know</u>

In much of the world today, knowing something has become synonymous with some level of proof. We have to "see it to believe it." We live in a context that visual demonstration is the final proof.

At the same time, we know how easy it is to deceive the eyes or the other senses. Nevertheless, we have trained ourselves to believe that knowledge comes through sight.

Intuitively, we also know that this is limiting and not true. Seeing and believing are two different things. There are things we see we don't believe or "know," and there are things we believe and know but don't see.

For example, if I watch a band playing live music, then I "know" that there is live music being played. If, on the other hand, a blind person standing next to me hears the live music, does he "know" any less than I that there is live music being played?

A few days ago, as I came through airport security, I heard music. Immediately, something about the dynamics and characteristics of the sound told me that this was live music. I questioned my thinking because I have never seen live music at this airport before.

Sure enough, I walked around for a few minutes, and there was a singer/songwriter with a small accompaniment rig playing live music. I "knew" the music was live before I saw anything.

Something about the characteristics of the music was so different from anything that's recorded that I knew long before I saw the musician that this was live.

Suppose a person who has neither sight nor hearing were in the same circumstance. Would something about the vibrations and their individual characteristics communicate "live music" to them so that their certainty and knowledge was equal to my own?

If I both see and hear the music being played and the performer who is making the music, is my knowledge "better, deeper or more certain" than a person who has fewer sensory inputs? If I have many inputs that demonstrate something, and I still don't believe it, do I "not know?"

Intuitively, we know there are senses and capabilities of our perceptual apparatus, both physical and spiritual, that go far beyond what we understand and take for granted as the "five senses."

"Knowing," is receiving enough evidence through some means, to make you certain that a thing is true. This includes things that are sometimes deemed "unknowable." Obviously, this definition presents several challenges.

In a world full of deception, where disinformation and outright lies is the norm, one could argue that it is impossible to "know" anything for certain.

If we live that way, relationships, business, and everything else grinds to a halt. Creativity vanishes, and our capacity to grow as human beings evaporate just as quickly.

Fundamentally, we all understand that there are many ways to "come to know." One way is through physical sensation; another way is through thought, yet another way is through connection with unseen forces, which are as real as the tangible and visible.

If knowing something can be defined in several ways, what about "not knowing?"

Not Knowing, Abdication, Uncertainty, and Resignation

One version of "not knowing" something is to give up, to run away, to abdicate. I decide that I cannot know something for certain, so I quit trying and give up the fight.

If I believe something is true and then pressure and lack of proof cause me to fear, it becomes attractive to abdicate that belief because I cannot "know" for certain. This kind of abdication is not the same as a willingness to live in "not knowing."

Another version of "not knowing" is to feel uncertainty. Uncertainty is usually tinged with some degree of fear. I'm scared about what might happen.

I don't know an outcome; I fear one or perhaps all the possible outcomes, so the uncertainty is not simply "not knowing," but is a fearful state of helpless anticipation.

A third version of "not knowing" is resignation. I believe I have no control over something, and I expect the outcome to be negative. I cannot see a way to influence the situation to create something different.

I don't want to hope or work for a positive outcome because I no longer believe it to be within the realm of possibility. I resign myself and wait for the awful news or the awful occurrence.

All three of these versions of "not knowing" come from the victim's mindset. A defining characteristic of the victim's mindset is "everything in the world is happening "to" me, and I have no power to do anything about it."

I am helpless and at the mercy of others, circumstances, and the universe. I live in a state of perpetual fear until the weight of disappointing circumstances calcifies, and I become a bitter cynic.

Therefore, knowing something is a choice to believe something to be true, however, the knowledge came to you.

Not knowing is none of the victim interpretations, but instead a condition of not having knowledge from any source to cause you to believe.

CHAPTER 17
WHO AM I?

Without trying to follow every possible combination of questions, it is easy to see that knowing something is a choice. You choose to know or not know.

Regardless of the number of inputs, either through the five senses, the other physical inputs we know exist but don't understand, or through metaphysical or spiritual inputs, we know when we choose to know.

In *The Book Of Context*, I described how we act solely on what we believe. At any given moment, what we think is or isn't true or possible, is the absolute boundary of what we imagine and create. In this same sense, we know something when we choose to know. We know something when we believe.

One summer, I took a four-day Grand Prix racing class at a well-known international speedway. The instructors were amazing, the cars were fast, and the experience was unforgettable. I learned to do things I didn't know I could do. Since then, driving has never been the same.

One technique was to use the gas and brake at the same time. You accomplish this by turning your right foot sideways so you can cover both pedals simultaneously. It had never occurred to me to try to use the principles of acceleration and deceleration that way.

This technique is essential for fast driving on a road with many corners because reducing the time between the application of gas and brake gives you more control and lets you navigate more corners at a higher speed.

It was weird at first, and my foot had no idea which to press. My intellect was completely confused, and I made mistakes. Then it became clear, and I could relax a bit, then a bit more even as the speed went up.

Living in a state of belief, balanced between knowing and not knowing is a powerful place. Imagine for a minute not being weighed down by the baggage of fear caused by "not knowing." Your mind moves fast, the decisions are clear, and the momentum is maintained, just like driving.

In saying that we know when we believe or that we know when we choose to know, I am not minimizing or ignoring the importance of sensory input. I see my socks are red and I know that.

I see the light is red and so I don't drive, and I avoid an accident. I do a scientific experiment and mix chemicals and create certain outcomes. Therefore, I know how those reactions work.

To know something through sensory input or experimentation is a valid way of coming to know things in the world around us. But it's a small and limiting path.

Knowing that comes from belief and choice is what creates great change. Great literature, political movements, personal heroism, amazing feats of athleticism, and astounding levels of spirituality are all accomplished by going down the path of learning to know through choice and belief.

When we limit our knowing to sensory input, we are one-dimensional and small. When we trust and learn to know as a product of belief and choice, we have limitless potential and can expand our opportunity for growth and influence to infinity.

The title of this chapter is "Who Am I?" Answering that question is the fundamental key to accessing the power to know through choice and belief. It is foundational to accessing power and certainty far beyond the limited scope of our immediate surroundings and our physical senses.

One way to answer that question is to appeal to biology. There is a notion that somehow our ability to be self-aware and be connected to the infinite, is the product of accidental, mindless and unintentional evolutionary forces.

There is a story told about a scientist in the 1800s who built a physical model of the solar system. It was a large apparatus with the sun in the center and the known planets orbiting around the sun. A crank turned to cause the movement of the bodies around the sun in the middle.

A friend of the scientist came and saw the wonderful creation. He exclaimed, "Amazing, that is a beautiful model. The motion is astounding, and it demonstrates so clearly what happens in the celestial realm." Then he asked, "Where did you get that?"

The scientist answered, "I don't know. I walked into the lab this morning and it was there. Perhaps it assembled itself from the dust and particles sitting in the lab. It wasn't there yesterday and overnight, it somehow came into existence."

The friend laughed and exclaimed, "Such a joke, you know that's completely impossible. I'm sure that you built it." The scientist looked at his friend and said in total earnestness, "That accidental creation is what you tell me happened to create the real thing."

Without debating creation theory versus "evolution," every person who reflects deeply knows that we came from somewhere. We have an innate sense of our divinity and the fact that there is organization and meaning behind our existence.

Answering the question "Who am I?" is critical for the creation of a life without fear. If you choose to believe and declare that your existence is accidental, has no purpose and begins and ends arbitrarily, then that belief governs the lens you wear in life.

If, on the other hand, you choose to believe and declare what you feel, that you have a divine origin, a purpose here in the world and gifts and talents to accomplish their purpose, then the lens of your daily experience is completely different.

In *Meeting God at the Door*, I described my near-death experience that happened in the summer of 2018. I came away with four essential and absolute truths from my conversations with God at the door between life and eternity.

These four truths I know for certain, without hesitation or doubt:

- Each one of us is a divine and intentional child of God.
- Each of us has divine potential and a mission or purpose in this world.
- Each of us has gifts and talents given to us to accomplish that purpose.
- All the help needed to accomplish that purpose and live to our fullest extent is available from both infinite sources and around us in the world.

Knowing that truth is the foundation for living without fear. Coming to know that truth requires belief and choice far beyond the limited input of physical senses. We have all felt those yearnings and feelings. Sometimes we ignore them. Sometimes we get angry and smash them when life doesn't go according to our wishes.

My purpose is to share that knowledge and encourage people to trust the intuition and feelings they have about their divine origin and purpose. Nearly everyone I talk to feels those truths at some level. Often it's difficult to talk about, and people don't want to express it because of fear of ridicule.

There is that monster fear again, showing up to rip the heart out of the creativity and possibility of each soul. Walking without fear is your heritage and your opportunity. Claim it.

When we choose to trust and believe in the narrow viewpoint of failure and fear, we lose hope and connection to power. The absolute truth is that the future is always unwritten. You create your life. Choosing, this moment, to live in that truth is the first step.

CHAPTER 18
WHAT DO I DO NOW?

I t's easy to say choosing to believe in your divinity, capability, and possibility is the important first step. Okay, so what? What happens with that belief? Like anything, belief is not enough. I can believe the sun will rise, and it will. If I do nothing with the new day, then it's just a sunrise.

The first step of *action* is to turn that belief or knowledge into a commitment. As I experienced the paralysis, the ambulance ride, the hospital stay, and the miraculous surgery and recovery, I knew the path was unfolding.

In moving forward with *Walking Without Fear*, my commitment to action was to live according to the knowledge of that divinity, capability, and possibility.

I didn't know exactly what that meant. I had to understand what I was choosing to believe and choosing to commit to. That led me to consider part two of this path.

What would it mean to embody that knowledge? What should I "be" as I live consistent with knowledge of divinity, capability, and possibility? I didn't know the answers, but that's okay because I was beginning to be comfortable in the space of "knowing" and "not knowing" at the same time.

After belief, the next step is "alignment." To act consistently with the principles of divinity, capability, and possibility, what thoughts, feelings, and behaviors do I want to change to move toward that alignment?

Those questions are hard to answer completely and fully. I found if I asked myself repeatedly during the day "am I thinking, believing and acting consistently with the knowledge of my divinity, capability, and possibility?" it was immediately clear in every situation with the answer was and if I needed adjustment.

The attitudes I held about things, the comments I made to others, the choices I made about what to think about, and what to focus on all shifted as I repeatedly asked those questions.

I was amazed at how fast clarity came by simply asking the questions and then trusting the immediate intuition about the answer. The more I thought and rationalized, the muddier the waters became.

The truth of our divinity, capability, and possibility reveals answers about alignment in an instant. You know intuitively whether your thoughts, feelings, actions, and intentions arc in line with your highest opportunity and the highest good of those around you.

The struggle comes when we start to rationalize things. The minute I heard myself saying, "but this is different...," or anything like that, I knew I was on shaky ground.

I turned it into a bit of a game. This helped defuse the self-accusation that automatically surfaced when I found I was not in alignment.

I got out of the hospital on December 14, and I knew the divine organized that. I had a few weeks over the holidays and during the beginning of the year to assemble the framework of what I had experienced and created a path forward.

In "Chapter 15," I described one of the conditions of my discharge from the hospital. I had to carry a bag of intravenous antibiotics for the next six weeks. This meant from December 15 through January 22, I had a big hip sack with a pump and a bag of meds.

Twice a day, the pump ran for three hours and put drugs in my body through a catheter inserted under my right arm, through veins across my chest to empty at the top of my heart.

These six weeks were a powerful reminder of the complete dependence I had on things outside my control. The home services people came twice a week to change part of the delivery system, replace batteries, and make sure everything was going smoothly.

I had never been tethered to anything in my life. It was a new and interesting experience. I thought every day about the question, "How is this experience related to living in alignment with my divinity, capability, and possibility?" This condition and my reflections about it led me to the third step of preparation in the framework.

I started with a commitment to live every day recognizing my divine origin, my mission and gifts, and the possibility this presented.

Regular questioning helped me keep alignment by making course corrections a dozen times a day to stay true to the commitment I had made. As this unfolded, I recognized a third element to this preparation.

That third element is focus. If I am scattered and trying to do too many things, I accomplish nothing. For example, if I worry too much about the weekly blood test, and the visits of the home care workers and the effectiveness of the antibiotics and the possibility of future infections and every other peripheral intrusion, nothing powerful would happen.

I chose instead to maintain a singular focus on what I was committed to being. This meant that every single day I lived in the truth of these three action steps:

- I have committed to living my life as a person who acknowledges and lives into my divine origin, capability, and mission and the possibilities that this brings to me.

- I choose to ask myself questions about my alignment every day so that I can joyfully change habits, thoughts, feelings, and behaviors that are not consistent with the truth.
- I choose to focus on my efforts on this singular purpose. I will be completely focused on learning, understanding, and then living life according to this truth.

Wow, when I read that now, it feels just like it felt then. It is an overwhelming thought. It feels large and out of reach. I took comfort in the fact that it also felt coherent and powerful.

I was certain that I was not going to be perfect or even very good at making this shift in my life. I tried to imagine what it would be like to live every day focused completely on the truth of my divine origin, the mission I only partly understand, and the possibilities that this creates in front of me.

Even though I felt overwhelmed, I began to feel a sense of purpose and peace. I knew that as I accomplished this, life would completely change. Things that were important before would disappear, and new energy would be my norm.

I also knew that I had just been through another life-threatening situation. This most recent dance was not as serious as the near-death experience six months earlier, which took me to the door of death. I still knew they were related and part of the whole growth process.

It felt a little confusing. I couldn't help but wonder, "If I understand and accept the truth of each of our divinity, capability, and possibility and then I commit to living that way, to realign myself regularly and to focus only on that mission, how many more gigantic obstacles and roadblocks will show up?

What did barriers, obstacles, roadblocks, illness, breakdowns, reversals, problems, and everything else that we experience signify if they keep happening even after I have discovered and live into these divine truths?

CHAPTER 19
THE GIFT IN EVERYTHING

The four truths given in "Chapter 17" are written with fire in my heart. I had experienced a visit with God in the summer and received those in a powerful way I could never doubt or deny.

I committed to three choices I described in the last chapter about how I live every day and from moment to moment.

I wandered through the valley of death a couple of times to get to this point. I knew my mission and purpose was to help as many people as I could understand these truths and achieve and express their divinity and gifts. As a coach, that is my sole purpose.

When a child learns to walk, they fall a lot. They don't think too much about it, they get up and keep going because they commit, even though it is unspoken, to learn to walk. Encouragement from siblings, parents and loved ones fuels these efforts until walking is a habit.

The bumps and bruises of falling are quickly forgotten as the encouraging love flows, and the thrill of a few steps erases the mishaps of learning.

What if barriers, obstacles, blocks, illnesses, accidents, reversals, bankruptcies, trials, and every other bruise and injury in our emotional and physical lives is a learning? What if I change the game and ask, "What is the gift," every single time something happens?

I remembered laying in the ambulance in staggering pain, paralyzed, tears streaming down my face and that somehow, after the vision of the Grim Reaper in the poker game, and making a fierce declaration to "call," I followed it up with the equally fierce question "What is the gift?" I don't remember why I asked it, except I knew there was purpose and power in the question.

The learning for walking without fear is simply that everything in life happens "for you." When we take the position that life happens "to us," we speak as a victim, and we memorialize our powerlessness.

When we accept the truth that everything is a gift and search for good things, we discover attitudes and opportunities we otherwise miss.

When you're angry or frustrated, you don't think clearly. You can't see the opportunity. That's true for you and it's true for me. When we calm down and choose to look at things as a gift and seek the opportunities, we find them.

There is a gift in everything. Leonard Cohen has a song *Anthem* that sings of cracks and opportunities. Hardships come, difficulties abound, things fail, and each struggle creates new seeds from old disasters. I love those lyrics and I love that song.

There IS a gift in everything. No matter how difficult, painful, undeserved or unexpected. The opportunity you have is to believe that truth and then look for the gift.

It would be easy to argue forever about this principle. An endless amount of energy and time could be spent on proving or disproving this proposition.

Choosing to find the gift demonstrates the awesome power of knowing through belief. The most powerful knowing in every area of life comes through belief.

When you change your beliefs, you change what is possible and what you can be and what you can do. You can argue about it, ignore it, or believe and act on the four principles of truth about our existence in "Chapter 17".

You can argue, ignore or believe and act upon the three action steps listed in "Chapter 18". What I've noticed is that energy and time wasted in such reasoning and argument never produce power and never brings someone to a place of *Walking Without Fear*.

Choosing the stance of finding the gift in everything moves you forward toward eliminating fear because it frees you from blaming, anger, bitterness, and lasting grudges against people, God or anything else as the complexities of life unfold around you.

The peace and space that this attitude provides cannot be measured. I have seen it in my life and the lives of countless clients. Leaving behind the need for recrimination, revenge, retribution, and justice is a freedom that's difficult to describe or understand unless you choose that experience.

CHAPTER 20
COACHING IN MY NECK BRACE

My emergency trip to the hospital was on Wednesday, December 5th. The midnight surgery was between the 5th and the 6th. I was in the ICU for the rest of the 6th and moved to to the orthopedic ward on the evening of December 7th.

I was on heavy-duty drugs for a couple more days and finally got coherent sometime on Sunday the 9th. My birthday was on the 10th. That gave me time to reflect again about what happened, my purpose on earth and the gift in this whole drama.

My normal coaching days are Monday, Tuesday, and Wednesday. Given everything that happened, I was in a profound state of reflection and torn between my mission and my need to recover.

I decided to start coaching again on Tuesday, December 11th. It might've been a silly thing to do; I don't know and perhaps will never know. Because of the wonders of the Internet, my iPhone and all the rest, I was able to do my coaching calls from my hospital bed.

Some people thought I was crazy and shouldn't be doing that. At the time, I felt driven to fulfill the obligation I had for clients. It had nothing to do with keeping my business running or earning money or anything mundane.

I felt a yearning to be the person I was called to be. I felt the drive to show up and "call" as I vowed in the back of the ambulance six days earlier.

Tuesday was exhausting. I couldn't do all the calls because it was too tiring, so I moved my group sessions to Saturday the 15th. I fully expected to create a discharge from the hospital on the 14th, even though that seemed unlikely. As I described earlier, that miraculous discharge was created, and I was able to fulfill the commitment on the 15th.

On Wednesday, December 12th, I got up early and showered and sat in a chair instead of in bed. I completed all the coaching calls scheduled for Wednesday.

That was exhausting also. I have reflected on that since and thought about what was going on. I didn't have a sense of trying to prove something. I didn't need approval from others. I was driven by a single thought. "This is who I am, and this is what I do."

During the weeks after my discharge, and while I was carrying my intravenous antibiotic bag, I did all the coaching I was supposed to do. Because I had decided the whole traumatic incident was a gift, I was determined to make the most of it, starting immediately.

For some reason, I decided that would happen best if I shared the experience and power with clients that I had at the moment instead of waiting for another week or two.

The coaching calls during those first days were powerful. There was a sense of both urgency and peace at the same time. There was an energy about them that was different, and my clients commented on the experience.

I call them clients because that's what they are. Truthfully, I have a deep sense of love and connection with every person I work with because that's how I choose to run my coaching business. The experiences of last summer and the previous weeks had only strengthened that connection.

I'm not suggesting it is important to do something like coaching in a neck brace or some other dramatic manifestation to walk without fear. I'm sharing what happened and what I did because this was the process of creating my understanding and framework.

What I discovered during the process is that my focus on preparing myself for the coaching calls and then completing those calls did two things: first, the days went by quickly. My mind was focused on preparation, delivering the calls, and then resting between calls so I could deliver the next one. The days moving faster made them more pleasant and fulfilling. Each day was a joy instead of a drudge.

The second thing I noticed was that my pain was almost non-existent during the calls. I can't say if it was less or if my shifting focus made me less aware of it. The net result was that I was in less pain, had faster days and had more fun.

Thinking about the three choices of commitment, alignment, and focus, make this outcome seem obvious and natural. I felt better than I felt when I was focused on my pain and recovery.

This was the blessing of coaching in my neck brace and living in the learning of commitment, alignment, and focus.

CHAPTER 21
THE MIRROR OF COACHING

One big benefit from my coaching practice is "the mirror of coaching."

I only have my life experience. I haven't lived as another person and can't fully understand what someone else experiences, believes, or wants.

This is true for all of us. This means everything we see, hear or come to understand is filtered by the lens of what we have experienced and what we think we know or believe.

This is obviously normal, but it presents a unique challenge in the coaching environment, where your goal is to be fully connected with someone else's world and understand what they are experiencing and feeling, through their lenses with their background and history.

As a coach, I train myself to listen deeply, listen to what is being said, and not my thinking about what is being said and allow plenty of space for ideas to formulate and develop.

I practice "removing myself" from the conversation and intentionally setting aside judgments and thoughts that occur naturally during the process of conversation. Listening in this way lets me hear and understand things that would normally go right past me.

Over and over again, I found myself hearing things from a client or saying things to a client that I know are important for my own life. In other words, I hear myself asking the question, "Kellan, are you listening?"

Some of my best coachings have come from my clients. It has come from my intentional development of love for them and my complete desire to hold space for them as they explore their own thinking and change what doesn't serve them.

The "mirror of coaching" means that my coaching shows me who I am being, what I am thinking, and what I believe is possible for my own life.

Another magic element of the coaching process is that we attract people who closely resonate with our life experience. That is not surprising given that we are shaped by our life experience and our beliefs about the meaning of that experience.

Claiming the power to shape your thinking and, therefore, your life experience is one of the fundamental discoveries of coaching. Learning to facilitate that process for others has helped me do it for myself.

Learning to listen deeply also makes me very receptive to words that get said by my clients or me. The words go in, resonate deeply and then show up for me later as reminders of what I might consider or do differently in my own life. In the coaching sessions that took place in the first few weeks after leaving the hospital, my awareness and sensitivity to this artifact of coaching was heightened.

Repeatedly, I felt like I was coaching myself. I knew that the dialogue benefited me as much as it ever would help my client. Because I spent so much time these first weeks in meditation and focused on the gifts of my recent illnesses, the coaching energy was powerful.

The fears of clients' hearts were coming through loud and clear. Fear of success, fear of failure, fear of embarrassment, fear of uncertainty, fear of not being "good enough," fear of not knowing what to say, fear of not measuring up to some standard, and every other variation of these common life occurrences. It wasn't that any of these were new, but I heard them all differently.

It rapidly became clear how much time and energy are expended because of fear. It blocks us at every stage of ideation and execution. Sometimes we manage it, and sometimes we hide. I was shocked as I thought through the number of ways that fear affects us.

For example, we experience:

- Fear of the fear that is coming,

- Fear as worry overtakes us,

- Fear each time something changes,

- Fear of feedback that might be negative,

- Fear of change,

- Fear of failure, success or any outcome,

- And on and on.

If you add up the time used to manage fear or think about failure and alternatives, it's overwhelming. What about the time and energy expended when things do go off the rails and you have to act and, at the same time, deal with your story about needing to recover from your "failure?"

In every conversation, it was obvious that there was a small or large element of fear that was preventing movement from where the client was to where they wanted to go.

This was true for every possible subject: growing a business, making more money, working fewer hours, creating a relationship with God, improving your family relationships, life meaning, personal fulfillment, career changes, habit changes, and every other goal that was on the plate.

This let me reflect deeply on how fear had affected my life. It made me starkly aware of the words I had spoken three months earlier about the effect of my near-death experience when I said, "I no longer feel fear."

How could I turn the combination of last summer's experience, this new dance with death, feeling personally vulnerable and diving deeply into the fears of clients into a framework of truly living life without fear?

CHAPTER 22
SURRENDER

As I deeply pondered the four truths from the conversation with God, and the three choices I made about commitment, alignment and focus, something began to emerge.

I had decided to seek the gift in every event, no matter the origin or the difficulty. Now a new level of awareness began to reveal itself as I put all this together.

I have read several books about learning to "trust the universe" and "let go and let God." That idea always seemed like something people said when they were too tired or too lazy to deal with the circumstances of life.

This was especially true when it seemed there were elements in people's problems that were brought about by their own behavior. Perhaps I was judging the motives and situations of others and not truly seeing the fundamental truth that was staring me in the face.

Like a math equation, the answer jumped out plainly. The first step to walking without fear was to surrender. Not give up but surrender.

Surrender in war means to accept defeat. You give up to save the lives of the soldiers that would otherwise be lost when you know you can't win the battle.

Surrender also might mean you no longer believe in your cause, and you judge it futile to continue to try to create some outcome. You stop trying.

Surrender in many other circumstances has a negative connotation. It means losing, quitting, giving up, resigning to reality, or some other euphemism that means simply "it's over" or "I quit."

Surrender in this context means to willingly and joyfully accept the truth and liberation that comes from acknowledging the following realities:

- There are four truths that govern who I am.
- I am divinely and intentionally created.
- I have a purpose.
- I have the gifts to achieve my purpose.
- I have help available if I seek and accept it.
- There are 3 choices I can make to activate the four truths.
- I choose to commit to my true nature and live accordingly.
- I choose a path of continual alignment with my nature.

- I choose to focus on the purpose I know I have.
- Everything that happens has a gift that blesses my life.

Some might say that surrender is a coward's way of living life. Some might say it doesn't allow you to seize the moment and make everything you possibly can out of yourself. The opposite is true.

Some might say it lacks personal responsibility and that by pursuing this path, you'll never know what you could make of yourself or what you can accomplish. Again, the opposite is true.

What I know from my experience is that when I did "seize the day" and "make the most of myself," I was wealthy and miserable. I destroyed opportunities and relationships. I was constantly afraid. When I chose to do everything according to my own thought and wisdom, I made horrible mistakes and hurt many people.

From my own experience, I know when I struggled in the world of seeking approval, I achieved it in great measure. I was viewed as a success by any measure from the outside. At the same time, I was lonely, depressed, in horrible internal pain and hated myself. When I fought fiercely for the right of self-determination without listening to my internal inspiration, all my successes turned into failures again and again.

What I now know from new experience is that as I surrender, I create more and better outcomes. I create happiness and wealth that is beautiful and consistent with what I know to be true.

The more I surrender, the more I am more myself. Far more than I ever experienced pursuing the ultimate path of "self-determination." As counterintuitive as it may seem, surrender is the ultimate "self-determination."

Surrender recognizes the fundamental truth that we all innately feel. There is more to this life than we perceive with our limited minds. There is a higher source of wisdom and power that is available to us if we seek it.

Making a conscious and intentional choice to surrender to my true nature is not an act of abdication or laziness. On the contrary, it is the path of greatest development, greatest joy, and most profound peace.

CHAPTER 23
OPPORTUNITY FOR GROWTH

As I meditated on this discovery, more truth flowed into my mind. Surrender was just the beginning of the process. The discovery of the power of surrendering was like finally finding the sign that marks the beginning of the trail that leads to the summit.

If I'm trying to find my way to the top of the mountain, I have to find the start of the trail. No matter how badly I want the joy of the view from the top until I find the trailhead, I'm just wandering around with the wish in my heart. I might try to blast my way through the bush and make it on my own. Anyone who has climbed a serious mountain knows how dangerous that is.

The name of the sign might say, "Surrender Trailhead, Summit 20 miles." Then a directional arrow would point out the path I need to walk.

In most national parks, there are brochures that describe the different trails that are available for those who visit. Trails are usually rated for difficulty and length. Often the descriptions also include sites along the way and what you can see from the top of the mountain.

If there were such a brochure printed about the "Surrender Trail," it would contain some of the following descriptions:

- Difficulty rating, extreme. Serious hikers only.
- Take plenty of water, dehydration and fatigue are likely.
- Be prepared for naysayers and discouragement.
- Take plenty of breaks, but don't sit too long, or your muscles will cramp.
- Keep going – the view from the top is incredible beyond all description.
- Watch out for detours and enticing distractions.
- Take some bandages and first-aid supplies. You'll likely have some slips and falls.
- Aid stations are located at regular intervals. Take every opportunity to stock up on supplies.

Each of us gets one journey through life. We know we came from somewhere else and brought experience and understanding with us. We all have a sense of knowing things from before and can't quite remember where or when. We all have the innate sense that there is something after we leave this place.

There are cynics who live with a "positive knowledge" that death is the end, and there's no future state. They are allowed to believe whatever they want, but it limits growth and possibility.

Arguments trying to prove one or the other are a waste of time. Living the one precious life you have following the intuition of what you know is true is the path for your greatest opportunity and development.

The things I have experienced have taught me the absolute truth of what I explain in the various books I have written. I know that this path of surrender, however difficult, is the path of growth and joy.

That doesn't mean that experiences aren't hard. It doesn't mean that when I fall and cut my leg it doesn't bleed. It bleeds, I need stitches, I yell at myself for falling, and I get mad at the rock that cut me.

At the end of the day, I seek the gift. I choose to learn and keep moving. I slow down when I'm tired and need rest. The motivation comes from the knowledge that I'm on the path I choose, and I know it's the right path.

What is the source of that knowledge? The knowledge has come as I choose to believe. The choice of belief is a certain path to the knowledge of all the important things in life.

We choose to love. We are not required to love. It is a choice we make in ourselves and we demonstrate the truth of our love by how we behave toward another.

Love cannot be measured or proved. It can only be demonstrated. It's the same with every other important aspect of life. Relegating knowledge to those things that we can "see" or "prove" in a laboratory setting is to miss the richness and nuance of what life has to offer.

It's to miss the meaning and purpose of our existence. We were not created to live in fear. Fear is the universal barrier. Instead, we were created to live in faith. Faith is the universal enabler.

Surrender is the greatest opportunity for growth.

CHAPTER 24
WHAT DOES THIS ALL MEAN?

The name of this book is *Walking Without Fear.* I wrote it to describe the journey I took that brought me to a place of living every day fearlessly and joyfully.

My goal is to share with you a framework to adapt to your own journey. The point is to get yourself to the same place if that's a goal you want. Imagine for a moment your own life, lived without fear.

I haven't lived your life. I don't pretend to understand or know all the things you know or to feel all the things you feel. That is impossible. I know we share the common human experience because we are created with far more similarities than differences.

I also know we each understand life through the lens of our experiences. There is no other way we can understand it. The limitation comes when we believe there is no other way to understand what has happened than how we presently understand it.

If we stay stuck in the mode that there is no interpretation for events and circumstances other than how we currently understand them, we are like the blind person touching only one small part of the elephant.

We believe there is only one way to understand this giant animal. It is according to the piece of the leg we touched. Forget we have not touched the ears or the trunk or the tail. Never mind it's much larger than we know at this moment. The only truth is what I know.

With that approach to understanding, we stay stuck where we are forever both individually and as a race. We would never make medical breakthroughs and would still be cutting people open to bleed out bad blood as a treatment for illness.

We would be stuck on a much smaller piece of the earth's surface because we still believe the world is flat, and if we go very far, we will fall off into an unknown abyss.

Growth as individuals and as a species come when we ask a very simple question: "What else could I believe?" Notice this is a reflexive inquiry. It is not helpful to ask what someone else could believe. It is always easy to see what someone else should do.

Most of us have stood looking over the shoulder of someone else playing chess or some other game. It is immediately apparent to us as observers what the person playing the game should do. We stare on in frustration wondering why they can't see the obvious.

If we trade places for a moment, we immediately realize in the midst of the game and the heat of battle, we can't see the same things we see when we are relaxed, nothing is at stake and we are merely observers.

Knowing this is true, what is it worth to learn the skill of stepping back and becoming the observer? What is possible if we learn the skills of meditation, reflection, and creating space so we can consider our own situations and problems from a different viewpoint?

If you choose to accept the truth that you are divinely created, then a corollary is that you have divine potential. That means your worth is infinite, and your creative potential is also infinite. However, just like developing any skill or capability to a high level, it takes a lot of work.

It would be illogical to assume that a high degree of development and the significant capability would simply show up one morning. No one wakes up a thousand times more skilled than they went to sleep.

Every piece of nature demonstrates the process of growth. It is gradual, slow, and requires the right inputs. You cultivate a beautiful lawn with good seed, good fertilizer and keeping the weeds to a minimum.

Our personal growth process is the same. We can spend a lot of time arguing about the principles or dithering about the choices. The outcome of that stream of action is a delay and lack of progress.

What this all means is very simple:

- You are a divine being with infinite potential.
- You have a purpose and design of your existence.
- You have gifts and talents to maximize that experience.
- All the help you need is available if you seek it.

You will recognize those as the four simple truths that came during my visit with God at the door between life and eternity. Those things are true.

The choice comes when we decide individually, one day at a time, sometimes one minute at a time, what we will do with those truths.

CHAPTER 25
THE LINE OF LEARNING

This all sounds interesting but from some perspectives a little weird. After the four truths, the three choices and the "Surrender Trail," where does it go? What happens next? OK, so I start trying to live according to that model, and then what?

Now we start the "Surrender Trail." Like the sign at the beginning said, there are aid stations along the way. Supplies, encouragement, and power are available to keep you moving.

That sign also says the path is difficult, littered with distractions and naysayers. It means living the three choices is a constant and perhaps difficult process.

I haven't played a ton of video games, but those I have played have some similar characteristics. There are always aid stations where you recharge your batteries, your protective shields, or get whatever rest and power you need. There are also enemies and traps and dangers that sap your life and block your progress.

You start a trail you know is hard and full of danger. Why would you choose to walk a difficult path when there are easier ways available? The truth is that most people choose an easier path. They settle for what is easy and obvious.

Most people live in fear because things are uncertain, scary, and they feel no control over what life brings them or how they are going to react to it. This is living defensively instead of creatively.

We all create coping mechanisms. Some live in resignation and bitterness. Some turn to practices or substances that numb the pain, angst or confusion. Some desperately pursue material success at all costs and then live lives without purpose or commit suicide because of the emptiness.

Most move along slowly and without a great deal of purpose. For example, there is a whole culture around "working for the weekend." Working all week, doing work we don't enjoy making money to have some fun on the weekend. Provided nothing bad happens, no one gets sick, the weather cooperates, and all the external things that could mess me up don't get in the way.

This is a typical "life without purpose."

I lived like that and I know many who do the same. Perhaps it is true of most. This fact is the very genesis of my personal mission. I was blessed to have radical wake-up calls and was given experience and transformation that changed my course forever.

The path of transformation, purpose, and joy is available for anyone who wants to go. There are no barriers at the beginning of the "Surrender Trail." Only warnings about the difficulty, the distractions and the preparation needed to stay on the trail.

I call the "Surrender Trail," the line of learning. It has five parts, illustrated below. They are sequential and each one leads to the next. It's easy to write down five words and then leave it at that. That would be equivalent to looking at the trail on a map. Then all my experiences would be just like another motivational book or speech.

What really matters is to get tools, encouragement and make a choice to create a life of meaning. The diagram below illustrates the line of learning. It shows the five parts of the path and how each step leads to the next.

The five Parts:

Surrender -----> Peace -----> Joy -----> Purpose -----> Power

The previous chapters gave the foundation required before I ever got to the place of surrender. If I had not known the four truths, I would have had no purpose and certainly not enough courage to understand that life is happening for my growth. I wouldn't see that all the effort I spend complaining about or fighting is a waste of time and energy.

----> move from theory to practice.

If I had not made and continued with the three choices, then surrender becomes scary and uncertain. Continual renewal of commitment, alignment, and focus is part of the process. Surrender without commitment, alignment and focus is giving up and giving in.

As I lived into the truth of "Surrender," everything changed. I got up every day with a sense of peace. Nothing was frustrating, and I was no longer afraid of what might happen.

I knew everything that would happen was part of the process, and I looked forward to each event — both the challenging events and wonderful events. The truth is, they are all wonderful.

If life is going great, it would be easy to explain having a feeling of peace every day. Given where I had been the last few months, it's easy to see how I could be anywhere but at peace.

As day followed day in a place of peace and with my commitment renewed daily, things changed once again. Instead of having occasional moments, hours, or even days of happiness, I found myself in a perpetual state of joy.

It is true that my wife's name is Joy, but this joy was riveted to my soul. I woke up every morning with it bubbling out of my lips and oozing out of my eyes. I was excited about what was coming.

At first, I found it a little strange to be living each day with peace and joy. I kept waiting for something to break and for it all to fall apart. It didn't.

As I realized this was a permanent opportunity, I wondered why it had been so difficult to get to this place? I struggled for decades with depression and incredible ups and downs. Now I found myself in a place of peace and joy.

"Why is it so hard to get here, and what would be required to live my whole life in precisely this state?" I realized only an understanding of how progression takes place on the line of learning would unlock the secret to move even further.

KELLAN FLUCKIGER

CHAPTER 26
THE FOUR LIFE THREADS

Because of the holidays and the lack of mobility imposed on me by my intravenous antibiotic bag, I had plenty of time to think and to write.

Reflecting on my life journey and the experience and journey of clients I worked with over the years, I began to see some common threads that were barriers to getting on the path of surrender and moving on the line of learning.

Another framework came to me and I saw it represented a common story for all of us. There are four threads that run through our lives. Four things we yearn for that make us happy when we have them and miserable when we don't.

The descriptive words each of us uses are different and the amount of each ingredient might be different as life unfolds, but like any recipe for disaster, there are lots of ways to create misery and failure.

These ideas have been given lots of names. I call them:

- The Thread of Connectedness
- The Thread of Freedom
- The Thread of Power
- The Thread of Value

The thread of connectedness represents how much we feel a part of something. We can be connected to others, we can feel connected to our divine origin or we can feel connected to a purpose.

A sense of belonging or connectedness is essential for mental health and productivity. There are documented stories of people dying from loneliness.

The second thread is the thread of freedom. It represents how much self-determination we experience. When we believe we have no self-determination, our productivity and power atrophies.

It's interesting to note that even people in prison have self-determination. Victor Frankl's book, written during his incarceration during World War II, demonstrated the indomitable power of the human spirit.

He demonstrated clearly that freedom of the mind is something we determine for ourselves. No one can take away how we choose to view ourselves and our situation.

The third is the thread of power. This represents how much we feel we can accomplish. What tools or skills do we have to make something happen? If we think we have no power, then we don't try anything, and life is colorless and boring.

As with all the other threads, where we are on thread of power is completely a choice we make. Power does not come from outside but from inside. Regardless of external position or title, someone may or may not actually have power.

We have all known leaders who have a title but no real power. On the other hand, we have known people with no title who wield enormous influence and can make all kinds of things happen.

The fourth is the thread of value. This is how much we think we're worth. If we believe we're worthless, then again, we try nothing, we do nothing, and we wither away and disappear.

When we understand that we have value, and we deeply believe that to be the case, all kinds of opportunities and possibilities open before us. There is no limit to what we can create.

We decide where we live on these four threads. This understanding is fundamental. All the threads are based on thoughts and feelings in our minds and hearts. We choose how we feel. We live in whatever truth we choose to create.

The Thread of Conectedness

Low   High

The Thread of Freedom

Low   High

The Thread of Power

Low   High

The Thread of Value

Low   High

The words "low" and "high" are used for illustration only. In the next chapters, we'll talk about the stew of misery we create with words and stories in our minds that keep us from choosing to create a powerful life.

If we live in fear, it's difficult to move from the low end to the high end of the threads because of the stories we have about ourselves.

Learning to identify old stories, realizing they are not true, discovering how to eliminate them and coming to accept the possibilities at the high-end of the threads is the key to moving through the line of learning, living life without fear and creating the kind of experience you wish to have.

CHAPTER 27
THE FOUR MYTHS

We have an endless loop that plays in our heads. When the rest of the music shuts down and the noise of the world is quiet, we have a background theme that plays incessantly.

This malevolent symphony is a little bit different for each person. Every single person feels and is unique. Their experience and how it sounds to them is certainly one-of-a-kind.

As I consider my journey through depression, addiction, and recovery and listen to thousands of others describe their own feelings, there are some clear recurrent themes.

We could have a long debate about where they come from and what should be done about that. That isn't the purpose here and maybe it doesn't matter. I am focusing on what to do with the discord and noise you have.

At the left-hand or the low end of each of the four threads are words that describe the painful ingredients of this background noise.

In the thread of "Connectedness," the low end is "Alone." We believe we are alone, isolated, separated, abandoned and left completely to our own devices as we stumble through life.

We believe that, because things happened which point us to such a conclusion. Sometimes there is actual abandonment. Sometimes the parenting style we received creates this. Sometimes the interaction with peers at school gave us that feeling.

For example, I wore clothes that were out of fashion. I frequently had patches sewn on my jeans so they would last longer. I wore ugly glasses. I looked like a nerd, I was a nerd and I loved the sciences.

It will be no surprise I got bullied a lot, called names a lot, got picked last a lot and felt very "alone." This happened all the way through high school.

Every person has their own version of these kinds of experiences. Some have many and some few. Even some who were popular in school and viewed as "having everything" often describe how lonely they felt.

In the thread of "freedom," the low end is "Trapped." Some combination of experiences taught you a "truth," you were stuck where you were. You came to believe you had no options and were trapped in the world you are in now.

For me, this was an artifact of the regular abusive punishment I received. I often considered running away but was too afraid to do it and didn't know where to go. I literally felt trapped and would sometimes scream into my pillow in frustration, not knowing what to do.

Events in all our lives have created some pieces of the refrain of "Trapped" in our disempowering symphony. The amount is different, but the notes are the same.

The low end of the thread of "Power" is the feeling of "Not Good Enough." Competitiveness at school, ridiculed by siblings, favoritism in families, and cruelty among peers are all contributors to this feeling.

At this moment, you can think of several things that would've contributed to some degree of this feeling in your symphony of sadness.

For me, that came from always getting in trouble to the point of severe punishment. For example, failing to bring home excellent grades, misbehaving in public, hiding broken things, etc. Loss of privileges, physical abuse, emotional abuse, and other things were heaped upon me when I didn't get things right.

I'm absolutely certain my parents thought they were doing the right things to get me to be successful in life – obviously, it had the opposite effect.

The low end on the thread of "Value" is the feeling of "Worthless." You'll never amount to anything, you don't have what it takes, you can't make the grade, you aren't worth saving and all the rest.

Intentionally or inadvertently, that message is stamped in large letters all over our faces by some events we have all experienced.

For me, this "truth" drove me to experiment with drugs at a young age – starting in the seventh grade. I was convinced that I was worthless and would permanently remain so. I was sure that I would never amount to anything.

Parental frustration was manifest in all kinds of terrible ways, even though I imagine they thought they were doing the best they could with a rotten kid. I remember one specific example of my mom telling me, "Up until you were eight, you were an angel. Something happened then and you have been terrible ever since."

It was not delivered in jest or even exasperation but in all seriousness and anger. You know right now the memory of certain things in your formative years still burns brightly in your heart and in your soul.

With these four words at the low-end, the four life threads now look like this:

The Thread of Connectedness

Alone   High

The Thread of Freedom

Trapped   High

The Thread of Power

Not Good Enough   High

The Thread of Value

Worthless   High

The purpose of recounting these myths is not to blame anyone or not to dwell on their power. We all know the power they have over our behavior in the present.

Unless…

Unless we recognize this and make changes to the old script. Every person has a symphony of sadness that plays. Some degree of each one of these elements is present in that stew.

The amount of each may differ, and the volume of this funeral dirge varies as days, months and years go by. Until we understand what's happening, recognize that it is not true and do something, it represents a powerful subtraction from our opportunities.

It is the fertile ground in which all our fears take root.

CHAPTER 28
THE FOUR TRUTHS

If you consider those four descriptors: "Alone," "Trapped," "Not Good Enough," and "Worthless," it's easy to see why fear dominates so much of our lives. Those are poisons that have no antidote if left to fester untreated. But they are myths.

What is the truth? If you look at a person born into the world and recognize the divine facts we talked about then we know each person is a divine child, with a mission, gifts and help to succeed, it is impossible for those four descriptors to be accurate.

So now what? Even if we accept the idea that the four scary words are totally inappropriate for each person born into this world, what is possible to combat the barrage of events and circumstances that give rise to the symphony of sorrow?

When I work in the recording studio and start to build a song, there are two ways that the work goes forward. First, sometimes I work on one part at a time. For example, I might work on just the baseline. It needs to have a certain feel and push to it, so the rhythm sits well in the groove I want.

The other way to work is after some of the parts are laid down, I listen to all the parts together and see where it feels crowded or muddy or empty. Ideas then come about what to take away or what to add to make the whole thing convey the message.

Getting off the bottom end of the four threads is about the same. It's not important to take life all to pieces and figure out exactly what past events created the sour notes in your symphony. That is like the endless hours with a shrink delving into the past.

Instead, If you sit quietly, what thoughts come about yourself? For example:

- I'm exhausted all the time
- I'll never make this
- What was I thinking to start this business?
- I see others do it, what's wrong with me?
- How come I can't consistently do anything?
- Why am I prone to fail?
- I'm just not cut out for... fill in the blank.
- Why am I so afraid of talking to people?
- I have too many responsibilities
- It's too late for me to do anything important
- This is just not the right time
- Maybe when I'm... (older, done with this, finished raising kids, out of school, etc.)
- A thousand other variations.

If that's the music you hear or something that sounds about the same, you know where you are on those threads. Without guilt or shame, it's important to understand where you are today.

What is the truth? Let's do them one at a time.

In the thread of "Connectedness," the truth is we are "Connected" and not "Alone." We are connected in at least three ways. We are connected to all the other human beings on the earth. We came from the same creator, and each of us has a purpose. Every one of us feels the most joy when we are serving others and adding good to the world.

In the thread of "Freedom," the truth is that you are "Free" and not "Trapped." The idea that your opportunity to choose has passed is nonsense. You are free at this moment to change every circumstance about your life.

Often, we use the copout "I have no choice," because we're not willing to put forth the effort or energy to make the change. But we all know people and have read hundreds or even thousands of stories about those who have simply made a decision and pursued a goal until it became real.

Every one of us is divine and has that power. There is no such thing as "impossible."

In the thread of "Power," the truth is we are "Powerful" and not "Not Good Enough." Every person has gifts and talents. Every person has the choice to develop them. Each of us is the master of our own attitude and belief.

I am not pretending that claiming the power we have is easy, or there would be no need to have a conversation about it. If it were easy, everyone would be doing everything they could be doing without any effort.

It is not only difficult, but it is obvious life is designed to be difficult. Even those born into "privilege," struggle with the same sad symphony and the same personal doubts and fears as those brought into the world in more difficult circumstances.

All this work is done on the inside and has very little to do with the external environment.

In the thread of "Value," the truth is you are "Important" and not "Worthless." In nature, all mammals protect their young fiercely. A "mother bear" is legendary for her ferocity.

Our natural inclination is the same. Intuitively, we know that we're important and only allow the circumstances around us to rip this truth out of our hearts causing that music to fade and the symphony of sadness to take over.

The four words describing the truth on those threads are "Connected," "Free," "Powerful," and "Important." It's easy to see that manifest in a young child.

Fearlessly learning to walk, crying until getting needed attention, sharing easily, loving without reservation. All those are the natural instincts of young children before they get contaminated with other words.

So now the four threads look like this:

The Thread of Connectedness

Alone	Connected	High

The Thread of Freedom

Trapped	Free	High

The Thread of Power

Not Good Enough	Powerful	High

The Thread of Value

Worthless	Important	High

We come into the world from our divine origin, wherever and however that took place, knowing that we are "Connected," "Free," "Powerful," and "Important."

Over time, a combination of experiences pushes us down to the low end of the threads. Well-meaning folks, along with those intending to do harm combined with the sad experience of failure, defeat, embarrassment and ridicule, stuff us into a corner of fear. From that place we don't try, we don't grow, and we don't build.

Even those who successfully navigate childhood, go through schooling, get great jobs, and move on into "successful positions," struggle with these same problems. Loneliness, divorces, drug abuse, violence and sadness in all forms flow from the fact that we still live with the symphony of sadness playing in the background.

We believe that we have no choice and that "that's just how it all works."

Nothing could be further from the truth. We were not designed this way, and it is not our legacy to live in such sadness. Likewise, it is not required to settle for what is easy and obvious.

It's easy to say the words of the "Symphony of Sadness" and then say what is true. How do we *move* from the bottom further up the threads? "Section III" shows how to make the change happen for you.

Getting to the truth in the middle of each thread is not the end of the game. It's only back where we started. Though we came into this world inherently understanding this, we didn't come just to get pushed to the bottom and then fight back to the middle.

Claiming your power and opportunity gives you control of your life. You are the creator of your life experience. You are the captain of your ship and the master of your destiny.

The only question is, "Will you take hold of the wheel and light a fire in the engine?"

CHAPTER 29
THE FOUR POSSIBILITIES

Accepting that our natural state of being at birth is one of "Connected," "Free," "Powerful," and "Important" is an important starting point. But it is only the starting point.

We didn't come to this world as an intentional creation to maintain the status quo. We didn't come in a state of innocent beauty with the intent of experiencing only the negative side of the threads and desperately clawing our way back to the middle.

Understanding what is possible requires three things.

Desire

The first requirement is desire. We must feel a genuine desire to have something we don't have right now. Whether we find ourselves at the low end of the scale or somewhere between the low end and the middle, we have an innate knowledge that more is possible.

However, knowledge only drives us when we allow it to flourish. If we crowd our minds with negative thinking and live in the symphony of sadness that occupies the low end of the threads, then knowing and wanting isn't enough.

Meditation

The second requirement is meditation. I'm not talking here about a specific discipline or type. There are many styles of meditation. Some require more discipline than others. Meditation, in this context, simply means the ability to sit still and learn to direct our thinking.

This sounds deceptively simple. It is simple, but not easy. It takes some guidance and a great deal of practice. I wrote other books on meditation, so I won't teach it here. Nevertheless, it is a critical tool to move to the high end of the threads.

The purpose of this meditation practice is to learn stillness. The world around us is full of clutter, clamor, and noise that demands attention. Technology and the pace of life crowd out any silent time or time for reflection. Creating that space is essential to moving up the threads.

Action

The third requirement is action. We must be willing to experiment with the possibilities to see what happens. If we allow fear to keep us crowded in the place of disbelief and inaction, we make a choice to stay where we are.

This right to choose is fundamental and foundational for any directed or intentional progress. Not choosing is choosing. Hesitation and waiting are choosing.

One outcome of my own experience with God at the door between life and eternity was a knowledge that choice is critical. Even with the four truths I described in "Chapter 17," and then again in "Chapter 24", the fundamental container for all this is your personal right to choose.

Regardless of your divine origin, the mission and gifts you have and the help that is available, each of us chooses whether we pursue those things or ignore them. We choose whether we listen to the yearnings we have or beat them down and live at the low end of the life threads.

If we have the desire, commit time to meditate to clear out clutter and take action, then we have clear vision and power to move our lives up the threads in a way that creates peace and joy.

At the top of the threads, we have the descriptors, "United," "At Cause," "Unstoppable," and "Precious." The threads with the complete descriptors look like this:

The Thread of Connectedness

Story · Born · *possible*

| Alone | Connected | United |

The Thread of Freedom

| Trapped | Free | At Cause |

The Thread of Power

| Not Good Enough | Powerful | Unstoppable |

The Thread of Value

| Worthless | Important | Precious |

Journey from the left to the right — all the help we need is available from the Divine & the real world.

Our connectedness at the high-end is when we are fully united. United with others, united with the divine and united with the purpose or cause that drives our fulfillment. There is awesome power in unity, and examples of that are all around us.

Teams together accomplish far more when individual players meld their will and their intention together and create something much more powerful than they can alone. This is true in sports, in business, and in life.

In the thread of freedom, it's one thing to be free and able to act for yourself. It is quite another to realize that you are "At Cause," and the architect of your life experience.

The deeper you dive into this thread through meditation, the more you realize that every aspect of the life you experience comes from what you think and what you believe about your thoughts.

In the thread of power, as you understand and use the power you have, you realize that you are truly unstoppable. Too often, we measure accomplishment only by a physical outcome. Just as valuable is the genius that creates powerful ideas that are not tangible.

For example, many complex mathematical theorems that relate to the fundamental forces of the universe are very difficult to explain or comprehend without difficult mathematics. Nevertheless, these discoveries allow us to do very tangible and real things.

Unstoppable is a powerful word. I intended to be so. The leap of believing that you are unstoppable is a chasm that few cross. It is possible and available. We will talk more about how to move up these threads in "Section III."

In the thread of value, the high end is "Precious." Without question, one of the most basic things people bring to coaching is a deep-seated fear that they really aren't worth much.

We can point to all our achievements and value creation as evidence to the contrary, but it is foundationally difficult for us to understand our own importance. Something in our early life experience or our daily "truth" makes that scary and hard.

I don't mean boasting about external victories. The quiet and bedrock truth is you are precious. Intrinsically valuable and worthwhile. "Important" is the baseline word that describes your state of being before you do anything.

If you add to your importance a willingness to serve others with your gifts, then you create value. Even with that value creation, becoming fully precious is not accomplished solely by creating things on the outside.

Precious is a state of being. A state of acknowledgment of your fundamental and integral importance in the grand scheme of eternal things. We have demonstrations of unimaginable love demonstrated by parents who rescue children, by soldiers who go to unbelievable lengths to protect others and first responders who risk life and limb.

This is not because it is a job. This is driven by a fundamental acknowledgment at the core of our beings that every life is precious. If we have distorted or stomped on this truth because of life experience, it is possible and desirable to do the work to uncover and live into this beauty.

Imagine for a moment living every day with the certain knowledge that you as an individual, are "United," At Cause," "Unstoppable," and "Precious." What would you do differently?

CHAPTER 30
FRAMEWORK FOR FREEDOM

This book is about "walking without fear." It is about living from day to day, driven by love and not limited by the blackness of fear.

A few years ago, I never imagined that I would live in this state of being, let alone write such a book. I never conceived of things that would happen to me.

Nevertheless, my path has moved me through these experiences, and I know what I know. My mission and purpose are to give this knowledge to every person who draws breath.

I can't require you to do anything, which I would not do anyway. But I do offer you both the path to creating your own life without fear and help in pursuit of your best self.

The framework might seem complicated. It might seem like there are a lot of parts, and it is difficult. It isn't. The parts are connected and founded on the basic truths.

In *The Book of Context*, I gave a process to change beliefs, one step at a time. In "Chapter 29" of this book, I said the first ingredient for change is desire. Desire is the precursor for belief. Usually, we just want something, and we don't believe in it yet.

It doesn't matter where you are now. If you start with desire, move to belief, and then take action, you can have what you are looking for.

To summarize all the pieces that have brought me to a place of living without fear, they're listed below and on a diagram on the following page.

1. There are four truths that I learned during my visit with God during my near-death experience. I know that I am not any different or better than anyone else on earth. In fact, it has occurred to me that I might be more thick-headed than most and consequently needed a bigger smack to wake up.

These four truths are:

o Each of us is a divine and intentional child of God.

o Each of us has divine potential and a mission or purpose in this world.

o Each of us has gifts and talents given us to accomplish that purpose.

o All the help needed to accomplish that purpose and live to our fullest potential is available from both infinite sources and in the world around us.

2. After the four truths, I was faced with a choice. I could do something with them or ignore them. We all have those fundamental choices. I knew that knowledge alone wasn't going to create the kind of life I wanted or provide the peace that had eluded me during my decades with depression. Consequently, I created three choices that govern my life:

o I committed to living my life as a person who acknowledges and lives into my divine origin, capability and mission, and the possibilities that this brings.

o I choose to ask myself questions every day about my alignment so that I can joyfully change habits, thoughts, feelings, and behaviors that are not consistent with the truth.

o I choose to focus on my efforts to this singular purpose. I am completely focused on learning, understanding, and then living life according to this truth.

3. Next is understanding that life has twists and turns. Our experiences take us up and down. I lived with decades of depression and had addiction problems. The story is in the book "Tightrope of Depression." For a long time, those stories an excuse to avoid creating the life I wanted.

Now I know everything that happens is a gift and each experience, no matter how difficult brings growth. I want growth, and so with everything that happens, I ask, "What is the gift?"

4. This brought me to a place of total surrender. Not abdication, not resignation, not giving up or thinking there is no hope. But a place of true surrender, knowing that everything is possible and I can create my own life.

5. Next, I realized the act of surrender was the beginning of a beautiful trail. I called it the "Surrender Trail." It has all the typical markings of a difficult journey, but like any beautiful mountain hike, the harder it is, the more beautiful the view and the more rewarding the destination. Here is the Surrender trail:

Surrender -----> Peace -----> Joy -----> Purpose -----> Power

By re-affirming my choices and living intentionally every single day, with plenty of patience for mistakes and mishaps, I found more peace and joy in my life than I have ever known.

6. Finally, in considering all my own disempowering stories and the themes I heard repeated with every client, whoever went on the journey of growth and self-improvement, I created the "Threads of Life."

I used words to describe things I felt. I realize everyone uses different words. I know if you quietly consider things that have prevented your growth, you will recognize yourself in these threads and the words that describe how they impact you. The four threads look like this:

The Thread of Connectedness

Alone	Connected	United

The Thread of Freedom

Trapped	Free	At Cause

The Thread of Power

Not Good Enough	Powerful	Unstoppable

The Thread of Value

Worthless	Important	Precious

When I talk to myself and clients about how to use this knowledge to create a better life, it is clear this is all a process. There is no sudden movement to a place of "enlightenment."

In my decades of meditation, I certainly had many experiences that could be described as "enlightenment." Periods of transcendent insight and transportation to an otherworldly realm of peace and wisdom.

Regardless of how frequently we have such experiences, we always return to the real world, the things around us press in and require attention. Old habits and fears are regularly ready to take over the stage without warning and without permission.

To live a life without fear requires constant choice and consistent work. Just like muscles atrophy without use, skills you develop in your mind and heart will get rusty without practice.

Daily, coming from a place of love, forgiveness, understanding, intuition, trust in the divine and all these wonderful sounding attributes is a choice. It is not an accident and it is not a one-time event.

Desire, which, when acted on, turns into belief, is the first ingredient. Developing a skill of meditation or the ability to connect with the quiet and the divine is the essential conduit. A willingness to act and act again and again is the motor that makes it happen.

This was the story of how I got where I am today. It is also the path I have used to help many make a similar journey. Adapt this to your own use and create your own place of peace, serenity, and certainty.

"Section III" will deal more specifically with practices and elaboration on this framework so you can apply it more easily and create whatever you want to have.

"There is great power in accepting who you really are."

Kellan Fluckiger

PART III
PEACE AND JOY AMID THE CHAOS

I t would be easy to in the book here and wish you good
luck in creating your own journey from where you are to
a place without fear. But that would be missing the hard
part.

Every one of us is an individual and has her own set of
circumstances, experiences, and stories that present barriers
to achievement and happiness.

I'm writing this section to give you all the help I can in
crafting your own journey. I will give you some tools I use
when I coach and some suggestions about how to adapt them
to your own use.

The other day, I listened to a podcast from someone who
had spent decades practicing meditation. I listened because I
have been a practitioner of meditation for over 45 years. I
wanted to share their journey and compare it to my own.

I started my meditation practice when I was 17 and got
interested in the martial arts. I continued with meditation off
and on my entire life. Partly as a safety valve to prevent my
suicide and partly because I truly enjoyed the calm and peace
that it brought to my being.

During my decades of depression, I achieved significant financial success, career success, and notoriety. I also lived with enormous self-loathing, ruined relationships, estranged family members and bitter relatives.

After finally starting my journey up out of the hell in 2007, I used meditation more diligently and with an intent to create my highest self and serve in the best way possible.

Because I was rescued by the divine from addiction and self-destruction, I owed a big debt. I was determined to be of service for the rest of my days.

That was 13 years ago. I had no idea I would have a near-death experience or the emergency surgery and brush with death I described here. I now realize all of this was preparatory work to move me along my own path of development.

My own experiences taught me everyone believes their path is the most difficult of any ever walked by another human being. That might sound dramatic, but when people who have struggled tell the truth, that feeling surfaces somewhere.

That's okay. Perhaps for you as a unique creation, your path of experience was designed to challenge and develop you in unique ways that only you can comprehend and appreciate.

Consequently, the last thing I ever do is try to get anyone to believe "it's not that bad," or "there are others far worse off than you." I don't know that.

What I do know is the processes and tools I have discovered and have given here, and in other books I've written, produce amazing results for those willing to take action and stay on the path.

Nothing happens without action. Nothing happens without commitment. The good news is that we all failed and fail repeatedly. Failure is as natural as rainfall. When we dare greatly, we fail greatly. The only answer is to get up, recommit and keep moving.

That glorious truth that keeps me moving on my path of development and excited and committed as I search for others on their journey that I might serve.

CHAPTER 31
FROZEN CONTEXT

This book is a sequel to *The Book of Context*. "Section II" of that book covers "Learning to Identify and Replace Beliefs." I refer to those principles as I assume you read that book. If you didn't, you should to understand the references and get the most value here.

Your context is the set of your beliefs woven together to form the boundary of what you accept as reality and think is possible in your world.

We all know, even in the same situation, different people believe different things. One person sees despair and impossible challenge. Another person sees an opportunity and starts creating a way forward.

The difference is the set of experiences each person has prior to the present. All our experiences from birth onward created a context from which they operate in that situation and every situation.

Besides the fact that I no longer experience fear, there is one other difference since my near-death experience.

When I talk to people, I see them in their "context." It's a bit difficult to explain, but It's kind of like a straitjacket that each of us wears.

A "context straitjacket" limits what we think about. It limits what we consider as alternatives or possibilities because our beliefs about what things mean are so strong.

When I describe it like that, it's easy to see how context limits every aspect of life. It limits our creativity, our relationships, our income, and our joy.

The other artifact of seeing people in their "context" is the "context straitjacket" that appears (to me) to be transparent and flexible. In other words, it doesn't appear as limiting.

Mostly, we don't believe our context boundaries are flexible. We don't "know" that. We live limited by the confines of that context straitjacket as we move through our daily experiences because it is what we believe.

We assign meaning to things, we make judgments, we do or do not try things, and we settle for the flow that our "context straitjacket" dictates.

The Book of Context was written to give a framework to change our context, one belief at a time. It contains a specific methodology to work on these beliefs.

Instead of attacking the belief directly and pleading or yelling at ourselves or trying to get someone else to convince us that our belief or "context straitjacket" is not correct, the method of change is based on experimentation.

Here are the four simple steps in that process. In any situation where you don't know what to do, find yourself feeling frightened, powerless, or lost, and you feel a determination to change, take the following steps with respect to the problem:

1. What do you believe? However ugly or limiting it is, make a simple true list of things you believe about the current situation.

2. What else could you believe? This is not a request to change your beliefs or an effort to convince you of anything. It is a simple question about what other belief is possible. Another way to frame this is, "What might someone else believe in this exact same situation?"

3. If I believed that alternative, what assumptions about this situation would occur? Pick one of the alternative beliefs you list in step two (that someone else might believe) and do the intellectual exercise of listing what you would assume differently about your situation.

4. Given the alternative belief and assumptions, what would I do? After you pick a belief, and list a couple of assumptions that flow, decide what you would do. If you have

played the game in truth and without drama, possible actions are immediate and obvious.

This exercise has three purposes. First, it separates you from an immediate overwhelming emotion of difficulty or impossibility by playing a game instead of focusing on the drama.

Second, you come to understand there are other ways to see the situation you're in, even if you don't believe them or think they don't apply. Third, you can create a list of actions someone with a different belief would take.

A simple illustration will help. I'm at a networking meeting, I'm afraid of people, and I don't want to make introductions. I list my beliefs which would include whatever self-doubts give rise to this context.

I know, without a doubt, others believe different things in the same situation because I can see them acting differently. I know if I had an alternate belief, I would act differently.

The question about action is simple. "If I believed everyone liked me and they were a friend I didn't know yet, what would I do?" The answer comes immediately.

If I *believed* that, I would introduce myself excitedly and without reservation. I would ask questions about them, be genuinely interested in their lives, and things would flow naturally from there.

It is always easy to pinpoint actions you would take if you believed something completely different than you believe to start with.

The experiment game then continues as you make a choice to take one of the actions. No expectations, no drama. You don't need to believe anything. Just take one action you specified as an experiment. What usually happens is you get an unexpected result.

The unexpected result is often different than the fear you had to start with, and that result then demonstrates the viability of a new belief. For example, you might make one great introduction and have a good conversation.

This spurs further action until changing the belief is a *consequence* of the actions and not something you mentally struggle with to create action.

That all sounds wonderful. Simple and easy to do, right? Not really. It is not difficult to understand, but putting it into practice can be tough. What if I can't think of anything that I actually could believe? What if every time I say something, I could believe the resistance is so strong I can't get anywhere?

Those are normal questions that come up a lot. This is especially true when beliefs are deeply held or have a lot of fear surrounding them. I call that condition a "Frozen Context."

A frozen context is where your context about a particular goal, opportunity or situation is completely limited by a set of beliefs you are unwilling or unable to challenge. Something has happened that has made it seemingly "impossible" to consider any point of view but your own.

This is often the case with trauma, significant childhood experience, and other situations where we are no longer aware of the events are shaping our views. We accept the limitations imposed by these beliefs as absolute and bulletproof reality.

One example was during my recovery and early treatment of depression. I had depression for 40 years before seeking any treatment. I didn't know what was going on in my life, only that I was periodically engaging in massive self-sabotage because of my conviction, "I'm not good enough."

That context was so firmly riveted to my heart and mind every time success would come. I burned it to the ground because I was certain I could not live in the place of abundance.

After some particularly traumatic events and nearly killing myself a couple of times, I sought help from a doctor and counselors. I experimented with a couple of antidepressants.

The key event was not the doctors or the antidepressants but a simple question.

My particular kind of depression manifested in a visceral belief everything around me that was "wrong" was my fault. If my wife or anyone close to me expressed displeasure, it was an indictment of my character and value.

If Joy would say something to me, I would immediately interpret it in the most negative way and be angry at myself for failure. Then the pressure would cause me to be defensive, and I felt frightened and then angry.

I hated how this played out, but it was the same time after time. One day, after she made some comment, not intended to injure, I felt the same attack. I ask in my frustration, "How else could someone interpret your comment?" "Any reasonable person hearing those words would know you meant to hurt and attack me."

She assured me this was not the case, and I was left to my own devices. Instinctively, I knew she was telling the truth even though it did not feel that way. I replayed the words she said in my mind and then I ask myself the question, "What else could this mean?"

When I spoke those words before, they were laden with energy, frustration, and emotion. If I repeated them with pure curiosity, and in a neutral tone, everything changed.

Suddenly, I realized that I could hear the words without emotional attachment or negative connotation about their meaning. If I simply asked what some words might mean, there were all kinds of ways I could understand the conversation.

The question "What else could this mean?" turned into a "non" drama inquiry where I realized the words might simply be a question.

It sounds simple to say, but the resulting shift in my context was immediate and profound. I realized the words might mean only what the words mean. I understood that my attachment of emotional meaning to them was from my context and not embedded in the words themselves.

That event shook me from a 40 year "Frozen Context." It happened because I was genuinely seeking escape. I was trying to understand what was going on in my life, seeking help, experimenting with beliefs, and doing everything else I could to create change.

My effort was rewarded, and the context shift was powerful and permanent.

The key learnings here are:

- A "Frozen Context" is not true, no matter what it seems like.
- A "Frozen Context" is not unchangeable.
- Regardless of how long your "Frozen Context" has existed, it is not permanent.
- There is a way.

CHAPTER 32
I CAN'T TO WHAT IF...

If you look at a "Frozen Context," it seems like concrete. Better still, concrete reinforced with rebar that is drilled into the ground 30 feet. It isn't.

The truth is, a context, regardless of how long you had it, is woven from a set of beliefs. You got these beliefs wherever you got them. Your childhood, your personal experience, your friends, your culture and the world around you.

One key to starting this process is to end internal fighting. End the drama. The goal here is not to gather enough explosives to blow up the brick wall. It is to let the brick wall evaporate.

An episode in the original *Star Trek* of the 60s had Capt. Kirk, Mr. Spock, and Dr. McCoy on a planet where they believed they were in the old American West in a "Gunfight at the OK Corral."

Wyatt Earp, Bat Masterson, Doc Holliday, and the Clanton gang members were all present. Everything seemed real except of course, this was impossible.

Outgunned and outmatched, Spock realized that the only defense was to come to a true belief the situation was imaginary, and the bullets, however real they seemed, would not harm them.

He performed the Vulcan mind meld and help them all come to that belief. The bullets ricocheted and blasted chunks off the corral fencing but did not harm our heroes in any way. They "knew" it wasn't true.

The skeptic will rush in and say, "Yeah, but they had a Vulcan mind-meld." True. Instead of finding reasons for failure, it is helpful to ask, "What is the equivalent mind shift you can do, at will, to change your "Frozen Context," no matter how real or terrifying it seems?"

Thousands of books and millions of hours of therapy have been spent on just such questions. Fundamentally we start with just one thought. All change begins with a single thought.

Every one of us has a giant capacity to imagine. We all have played games as kids or adults where we imagine circumstances that are completely different from our "reality." The magic of movies, books, music and art demonstrates the unlimited nature of the imagination.

Somewhere along the way, we lost our ability to truly imagine. We simply accept our thinking something won't work, can't be done, is impossible, or is just out of reach.

Let's start with a very simple shift. You know the feeling in your gut when you feel "I Can't." It's a sick feeling, a sadness, a certainty. Some combination of things that spells "FEAR."

If you are willing to accept the idea that even the most severe "Frozen Context" can change, then every time you have the sensation of "I Can't," immediately answer with a question of your own.

"What If...?"

CHAPTER 33
LIBERATION EVENTS

A "Context Straitjacket" is imagery to describe a set of beliefs that have us locked in a place where we live in the certainty of what we cannot have, cannot be, or cannot become.

One framework I use for coaching is "Break the Cage." The cage is an equivalent metaphor that represents the feeling of being confined or trapped or unchangeably fettered to some present reality.

Some have likened this to being in jail, some have likened it to being under a magic spell. All these metaphors are descriptions of a situation where some mental construct is limiting us in ways that are not true and not necessary.

The limitation is true and real, but only because we allow it to be. If we had our "Vulcan mind-meld," a counter-spell or the key to the prison door, we would be free.

The example I gave in "Chapter 31", where I finally *really* understood there were many ways I could interpret the same words, was a "Liberation Event" for me.

When you find yourself at the low end of the four threads, we described earlier, you know, without question, that you are stuck in a "Frozen Context." You are locked in a cage and in need of a "Liberation Event."

There are five things required to create a Liberation Event:

1. Moment of Inspiration.

2. Commitment to Create.

3. Plan for Change.

4. Source of Continual Power.

5. Process for Consistency.

A moment of inspiration might come from many places. For me, it came from deeply considering my own question to Joy. It might come from a book, seminar, a coaching conversation, an answer to prayer, meditation or a hundred other places.

It is a feeling that is powerful and makes you "know" (and believe) that something else is possible. There is something higher and different that is truer than the context you have now.

Some version of this inspiration happens to us regularly.

Unfortunately, we generally ignore it, write it off as impossible or let it sit there until it fades and becomes yesterday's news.

These moments of inspiration generally come easier and more powerfully when we are seeking. We have decided something must be different, and we are actively pursuing a path to a new place.

Occasionally a flash of insight may come "uninvited." Whether by surprise or due to diligent seeking, the inspiration is useless without an immediate commitment to do something with it. Enthusiasm and excitement have a shelf life. If you don't start right away, the excitement fades, and the dream gets stale.

Commitment only comes from one place. It is a choice you make on your own because you decide you want something and will pursue it at all hazards. People can encourage you, command you, threaten you or bribe you. Without a firm internal choice and a commitment to do the work, nothing will be different.

The plan for change is required to make something materialize. Such a plan can be complicated or simple, depending on the need. It must address a process for institutionalizing what you saw as different in your inspiration.

For example, in the situation with Joy, where my moment of inspiration changed 40 years of context, I sat thinking about the question and its implications for a couple of hours. When realization there were more possible ways to interpret the words soaked in deeply, I got excited.

I considered other circumstances that previously felt the same. Times when I heard certain words and was convinced the speaker and the intent were negative. My plan for change was simple.

Every time I have a rising negative emotion, which I gave the name "feeling like sandpaper" (it felt like someone rubbing my eyeballs with sandpaper,) I committed to stop and ask myself the same question: "What else could this mean?"

That plan of action was sufficient to get started. I just had to keep it. Other pieces would be added as my growth has progressed.

A source of continual power was necessary to help me keep it. Change can be both physically and emotionally exhausting. There were times I didn't feel like going through the mental exercise of wondering how else to interpret the world around me.

My source for continual power came from three places. I treasured the feeling I had when I first realized there was another way. I love that feeling and wanted it to continue.

Second, I knew Joy was all in to help me get better and reframe my life. Third, I knew God was interested in my success.

I didn't have a coach at that time, or my other source of power would've been talking to my coach and discussing situations that came up where I wanted insight and support.

The fifth step, a process for consistency, is a commitment to be held accountable. When you're married, sometimes it's difficult to use your spouse as an accountability partner. Joy was willing, but sometimes it worked and sometimes it didn't.

My best sources for accountability are my coach and my relationship with God. The key was not forcing. Neither my coach or God were interested in forcing me to do anything.

The key was my true willingness to change my "Frozen Context" immediately and permanently. Success was slower than I wanted, but my determination never wavered.

Despite failures and setbacks and fabulous belly flops, I was able to completely eliminate the old belief and the limiting effect it had on my context and my life.

It all starts with a desire to change. You choose to ask, "What If...?" Then you look for inspiration and moments of insight. You find them in meditation, books or most effectively, working with a coach.

You make a firm commitment and resolve to continue. There are no bands playing and no parade. It is just a choice you make without reservation because you can. You are the architect of your life.

You create a plan to keep the seed of change alive and growing no matter how small it feels to start with. You intentionally seek out and access sources of power to keep you supported. You enlist and agree to an accountability process. Not because you have to, but because you *want* to.

CHAPTER 34
THE FOUR QUESTIONS

Fear is an unreasonable monster. It strikes without warning and the grip can be fierce and unrelenting. It's easy to talk about ways to manage fear or to banish fear, but they don't always work.

Whether your fear is about one particular thing you face or the doubt about creating a "Liberation Event" to make a major context shift, fear can be a significant barrier.

I have four questions to help me form a realistic view of fear that shows up in my life. The first question is, "What exactly are you afraid of?"

It is easy to brush this off and say, "I don't know." In fact, that is the all-encompassing copout that escapes our lips when we are unwilling to spend a few minutes thinking about the question.

Fear is much more powerful when it remains an unnamed, nonspecific, and nebulous mass of unexplained terror that grips your stomach or your heart.

We often know such fear is unreasonable. That doesn't make it any less powerful. So sitting with the question "What am I afraid of?" is a useful exercise. You might need to sit with the question for several minutes until you are willing to start listing what comes to mind.

Common fears are:

- I don't know what I'm doing.

- I'll be embarrassed.

- I'll look stupid.

- People will laugh at me.

- People won't like me.

- I will be exposed.

- I will be abandoned.

- I will be lonely.

- I just can't do this

I often start by acknowledging the truth. Maybe I don't know exactly what I'm doing. Maybe I will be embarrassed. Maybe I will look stupid and somebody will laugh. So what? What is actually the worst that can possibly happen?

I am an experienced public speaker and generally have no issue in front of a crowd, cameras or microphones.

One particular speech was scheduled in front of a group of people who I thought might know embarrassing details about my background. I had a secret fear of being heckled or laughed off the stage as an imposter.

My coach at the time asked me, "What is the worst thing that can happen?" I didn't fear actual bodily harm. I thought seriously for a moment and said, "They will chase me off the stage with pitchforks and torches." I was partly joking, but we ran with it.

He said, "Okay, let's assume they do. Then what will happen?"

"I will go home and go on with my life."

"Will you die?"

"No."

"Will life go on?"

"I think so."

I came to realize nothing would *actually* happen. The worst fear I could imagine would result in nothing at the end of the day. The speech went off without a hitch, and I got invited back.

The second question is, "Why are you afraid of that?" It is one thing to list fears. We act like when we say, "I'll be embarrassed," everyone simply knows without question why that is a totally undesirable outcome.

In truth, it depends on the context. Describing why something scares you is a valuable exercise. If you fear being embarrassed, and you think about why it brings up related statements like "people won't like me." "I will lose credibility."

Stating the why behind each of these fears reduces their power. Such a thread might look like this "I will be embarrassed, then I will lose credibility, then I will not get promoted, then I will be fired, then I can't get a job, then I will starve, then I will die under a bridge."

Simply walking through the trail almost always gets to someplace that sounds ridiculous on its face. Often it goes back to some event in childhood that has stamped a memory deeply on your heart.

When you say all this out loud, and listen to what it sounds like, it often loses power and shrinks. That allows you to put your fear in proportion to what's really going on.

The third question is, "Is it true?" In other words, do you know with a high degree of certainty or with absolute certainty the thing you are afraid of will happen or the subsequent consequences will manifest?

By this time in the questioning process, you realize the answer is almost universally "no." We actually have no idea what's going to happen. Walking through these three questions is often enough to either eliminate the fear or shrink it to a manageable size so you can discuss how to do whatever is in front of you, instead of being paralyzed by why you can't.

The fourth question is, "What do you believe that gives this fear power?" This question can take some time and may go deep into past events.

If you're working on creating a major shift or finding a "Frozen Context," then you might visit this question several times in different emotional states so you can have a good view of what's going on inside.

In *The Book of Context*, listing beliefs is the first step to changing them. If you create a list of beliefs that you are not happy with, then the four steps to begin that change would start here. Truthfully describing what you believe, however it might sound when read out loud, is helpful for two reasons.

First, making a list requires that you think deeply about what you believe. This is especially true when beliefs are nebulous or deeply held. When it stays formless, it is stronger. Second, you move things out of the nameless realm to concrete words and meanings. When you hear yourself speak the words, you can decide if what you are speaking is true or just old history.

CHAPTER 35
YOUR CORE CONTEXT

Many studies have shown our first five to six years of life, form most of our personality. Personality is the combination of characteristics or qualities that form an individual's distinctive character. Personality is difficult but not impossible to change.

"Core Context" is the set of beliefs, expectations, and possibilities you "know" are true about yourself, others, and the world around you. Core Context begins forming during the same period. It extends beyond early childhood to include major events up through the teens.

The older we get, the more we tend to experience events, even traumatic ones, through the lens of our "Core Context," instead of having those events influence the context.

We interpret others' behavior, events in the world, and our own achievements or misfortunes in the context of what we believe is possible and available. We begin to settle into "that's just how it is."

In understanding my core context, I noticed certain types of events, some traumatic, some mundane, that shaped my view of myself, others, and the world.

I received brutal and inconsistent punishment for a variety of offenses at home. I never knew when the next time I would get smacked was coming – I only knew it would be soon.

Perfection was the standard. Less than great marks at school were not tolerated and often, but not always, rewarded with severe consequences.

As a bookworm and social outcast at school, I had nowhere to feel acceptance and belonging. Not unexpectedly, I turned inward to books and make-believe worlds.

I believed my parents were perfect, that their parents were perfect, religion was perfect, and there was no way I would ever measure up.

I was prohibited from normal friendships in the neighborhood and even with others in the same church because they weren't behaving in a way that was "good enough."

There were similar limitations, and the common thread shaped me with a core context that "I was not good enough and never could be." "I will be lucky to measure up and get by in the world."

"I am unworthy of friends and will be lonely." "I have to prove I'm okay everywhere I go and do something extraordinary, or I will disappear."

"Everybody else always gets the good stuff, and I get leftovers and emptiness." "I have to lie in order to keep myself safe."

You will recognize all these and their hundred variations from "Chapter 27" on "The Four Myths." My core context put me firmly at the left end of those threads.

After decades of depression, a great deal of effort, attention, and focused work have changed my core context to one of "Freedom, Prosperity, and Joy." It took so long because I didn't get help.

I didn't realize how broken my worldview was and believed it was all my fault anyway. As I have done the work and made internal changes, I recognize the language and behavior of many who live far below their possibilities because they, like me, swim somewhere in the symphony of sadness.

What is your core context?

Make a list of the fundamental things you believe about yourself, the world around you and your opportunities. Be completely honest so you can create a good picture of how you view things.

My Core Context was extraordinarily negative. Yours may also be negative, or somewhere else on the scale.

The point of this thought-exercise is less about where you are at this moment than about verbalizing these beliefs so that you can *understand* where you are.

The power of this introspection comes because knowledge of these beliefs helps you understand why you react the way you do to people, circumstances, and events and what beliefs are keeping you stuck where you are.

With this understanding and using the four questions in "Chapter 34", you can make an intentional and significant change to the context you have. Because your context is woven from beliefs, it is subject to change. Your opportunity is to make conscious decisions about changing your view of the world.

The question "What else could I believe?" Suddenly takes on tremendous importance and power. You truly are the architect of your future.

"People complain about "freedom."

The truth is, freedom is fearful, the limitations of the familiar create far too much comfort..."

Kellan Fluckiger

CHAPTER 36
FEAR VS. NOT KNOWING

It is important to revisit the meaning of "not knowing" we talked about in "Chapter 16". Not knowing is a safe place. Fear is the place closest to death.

Not knowing is an acknowledgment of opportunities not yet seen or understood. Not having control and being afraid is another manifestation of not believing.

If one part of your core context is "every time I don't know something, it turns out bad," then not knowing is equivalent to fear. Another view is, "every time I don't know something, there is a surprise waiting for me."

Resignation, abdication, and paralyzing uncertainty are the destructive faces of "not knowing." Commitment, creativity, and clear vision also come from the state of "not knowing."

Your interpretation of "not knowing," determines the feelings associated with this condition. Not knowing a next step or a likely outcome is not frightening if your context includes the certainty everything happens "for" you and not "to" you.

Regardless of the events that formed your current context, your context is formed from beliefs *about* those events. For whatever reason, you accepted those beliefs before this moment. You can continue to accept them or make intentional adjustments.

The old example of the elephant and the string comes to mind. A baby elephant is staked to a chain which it cannot escape regardless of how many times it pulls to get free. As an adult, the elephant is held in place by a string because of belief it is unbreakable.

Our context functions in a similar way. We believe we are enlightened and would not be held captive by such fallacious thinking. Nevertheless, we see it manifest around us all the time.

We don't believe something can come true, so we don't try. We "know" a certain effort will fail, so we don't even start. After all, it's always been that way. The examples are too numerous to mention.

With absolute certainty, that comes from my experience with God at the door between life and eternity, I know the reason we do not achieve our capability is that we don't *believe* we can.

One possible view is to argue with that premise and explain all the reasons it is untrue. That behavior demonstrates a "Frozen Context."

Another more empowering course of action is to laugh at ourselves for being held captive by a string.

Immediately understanding the incredible vistas before us and the infinite capability of our creative souls is a lot more fun, empowering, and starts to produce real results.

I don't know the capabilities you have. I do know most people settle for the easy and obvious because of the limit of their context. Don't let that be you.

CHAPTER 37
WHAT IS HAPPENING IS NOT YOU

One frequent confusion that hides the truth and hijacks our desire to change is allowing external events to define beliefs that weave our context.

One example with far-reaching consequences is children who blame themselves for their parents' divorce. A relationship fails for many reasons. Children don't understand what's happening and assign blame to themselves.

They believe their own failures, actions or inactions caused the trouble and that somehow, if they are "good enough," the trouble can be repaired. This terrible circumstance is made much worse when separating parents start using the children as pawns in a power struggle.

Long-term emotional damage is done, and extreme context shaping takes place in the children when this happens. The consequences of this shaping will influence the child's life until some liberating event helps them change the context.

Another obvious and terrible version of this is a woman who stays in an abusive relationship because she believes she somehow deserves this treatment.

Alternatively, she might believe nothing better is available, and that is "just how it all works."

No clear-thinking person would agree with either the child or the abused woman. Yet we see this over and over again. Significant counseling and enormous expense might be required to repair the damage from these situations.

Every single person lives with hundreds of such false beliefs. We have adopted and accepted stories based on old experiences. We then "believe" these cause-and-effect relationships are true and nothing different is available.

One example for me happened as a senior in high school. I was asked to perform a piano solo with the band. I practiced for months and was as prepared as I knew how to be.

The performance went well, except there was one section when I made a number of mistakes on the piano. I wanted it to be perfect and it wasn't. My high school band director was also disappointed and made a comment "it's only high school." My mother was also disappointed. The two people I wanted to impress were disappointed. I was clearly a loser.

From this circumstance, I took away a disempowering belief. "You can practice all you want, but the final performance is a crapshoot and might be good or not, so, just hope for the best."

This "truth" affected my performances for decades. Unreasonable fear far beyond stage fright, unnecessary drama, and debilitating depression kept me from doing my best.

My belief limited my capability. Today, I know performance is under my control. I play the piano absolutely as well as I have prepared. Mistakes are not random and are subject to appropriate technical and mental preparation and focus.

For many years, my ability to contribute my gifts and talents, enjoy music, and do what I wanted to do were limited by a false belief. That is not true today, but I can't retrieve the lost years and I cannot undo all the terror I felt as I prepared for musical work over the years.

There are thousands of examples of similar limitations I have helped clients resolve over the years. Learning a new "truth:" what happens around us does not define us, and undoing limitations caused by long-standing beliefs is a big element of the coaching work I do.

What beliefs do you have that limit your opportunities? Are you ready to do the work to change them? Unlimited joy and contentment are just around the corner, waiting for you to collect them.

CHAPTER 38
TRUSTING THE DIVINE

There comes a time when it's necessary to make a choice about belief. In fact, this choice repeatedly comes until believing is your natural state of being.

The idea of "surrender" is not "well I'll try this and see if it works for me and if I prove it's correct, then I'll believe and surrender a little bit more." When we have a fierce illusion of clinging to control backed by fear of what happens when we don't control, that is how we approach belief.

In the ambulance, when I had the vision and shouted my determination, "then I call," it was the first of many times I affirmed this truth. It was not a resignation, a giving up or a fearful belligerent outcry.

It was a firm choice and fierce determination to stay true to what I knew from my previous experiences and move forward with clarity and belief in the future.

The four truths stated in "Chapter 17" and again in "Chapter 24" are true. I can't change them. What I can do is ignore them and make them inoperative in my life. That is the fundamental choice we all face.

We know the yearnings and desires we feel, and we know when we are ignoring them and when we are heeding them. With practice and with intentional listening, it becomes even clearer.

Learning to walk without fear means relinquishing control. It is an illusion anyway. The more fiercely I cling to the need for control, the more powerfully fear derails me, clouds my vision and limits my options.

The truth of trusting the divine is not abdication and giving up. It's a recognition of the order of things in the universe and of the glorious powerlessness of each of us.

I say glorious powerlessness intentionally. It is glorious because the truth is there is divine purpose. There is divine intention behind the creation of each of us. We are children of God. We have purpose and meaning.

We have gifts and talents to develop and express in our lives. There is a divine order and path that each of us can walk *if we want to.* The "if we want to," is the critical determining factor.

Do we want to a little bit, once in a while, and only when it's convenient or do we really want to? Are we willing to trust the divine and surrender to the inspiration and intuition that we receive?

Are we willing to work and develop our sense of intuition and inspiration until it is trustworthy and reliable, and we know what it sounds like?

Are we willing to act on that inspiration and intuition, regardless of understanding the outcome ahead of time, and even when it leads through difficult experiences or up rocky paths? What about when the dirt beneath our feet becomes unstable, and we slide down the mountain?

Trusting the divine is a decision we take over and over again. That is the true meaning of surrender. it is a positive, uplifting, liberating, and glorious opportunity.

Trusting the divine and walking the "Surrender Trail" leads to peace of mind and certainty in the heart. These things are not instantaneous, or they wouldn't provide many opportunities for development. On the contrary, it is a learning process and mirrors the path of growth, followed by every element of creation.

Chapter 39
Core Context Shift

You now know what a "Core Context" is. You know how it is formed. If you think about things that have happened to you and match those up with your beliefs about the world around you, the behavior of others and the opportunity in front of you, you know the shape of *your* "Core Context."

You know what a "Liberation Event" is. You have felt the yearning to create such an event at various times. A deep longing to change something fundamental. A "knowing" that something could be different, combined with the desire to make it different.

A liberation event is only the beginning of such a change. In "Chapter 33,", I identified the five key pieces of creating a liberation event. They are:

1. Moment of Inspiration.

2. Commitment to Create.

3. Plan for Change.

4. Source of Continual Power.

5. Process for Consistency.

Those five parts are the start of a core context shift. The moment of inspiration is recognizing a yearning of possibility. The commitment to create is a choice you make to do something with it.

The plan for change is required, or nothing will be different. "If we always do what we always did, then we always get what we always got." The plan for change is our map to make the commitment from Step Two into reality.

Any change in your heart, in your mind, in a relationship, in your finances, or anywhere else in the real world, requires effort and energy. Therefore, the fourth step is a source of continual power. The obvious source is your own determination and your connection to the divine.

Every single person has ups and downs. Each of us can learn to take control of our thoughts and emotions, particularly when things are difficult or when outcomes are different than we planned.

Such setbacks are no different from a tree having a dry year or encountering rocks as the roots go down into the earth. Alternatives must be created. Adjustments must be made. But the determination and the commitment remain the same.

The process for consistency is something you intentionally develop to keep moving. Where will you turn for counsel, encouragement, ideas, and reassurance of your own worth and the value of the outcome you seek?

The core context shift comes as a result of the relentless execution of your plan for change. I cannot tell you exactly how you will achieve your own core context shift. I can share with you what I did and how I help others make this fundamental and life-changing shift.

As a coach, I have developed frameworks and tools that I use and share with clients to create fundamental shifts in how they view the world and, consequently, what they accomplish.

Before I was a coach, I used the same processes in a less rigorous way. I was devoted to daily preparation through prayer and exercise and learning. I tried different methodologies for meditation and personal enlightenment.

The key was consistency. That doesn't mean you never miss a day or fall off of the commitment wagon. It does mean renewing determination and recommitting when changes or detours happen.

In my coaching, I developed the "Break the Cage" framework. CAGE is an acronym that stands for two different lists, depending on where you are in the process. When you find yourself stuck in a core context that is disempowering and your beliefs are holding you hostage, then the acronym stands for:

- Compare
- Abandon
- Grumble
- Excuse

In a place of lack, we are always comparing ourselves to others, and we feel good only when we come out on top in that comparison. When the comparisons go poorly, we abandon our hopes and dreams and retreat inward.

Then we grumble about the difficulties of life and how the world or our situation is unjust. Finally, we excuse ourselves because, after all, "it's not our fault and all the breaks have gone against us." And if only "they" out there would be different, everything would be okay.

Obviously, this is not true and is an abdication of your true power. It represents living on the low end of the four threads. When you take control of your life, make the changes you choose in your core context, then the acronym changes and becomes:

- Create
- Achieve
- Grow
- Enjoy

From this place, life looks completely different. Even when things don't work out or setbacks occur, the core framework of trusting the divine and seeking to discover, develop, and manifest your Divine gifts and talents keeps you moving. I have a book titled *Break the CAGE* already in the works.

Another framework I created is called "The Results Equation." I have a book by that name as well. This framework gives a step-by-step approach to accomplishing any goal.

The framework is universal and adapts itself well to both internal and external targets. There are many other frameworks and tools I and others have created available to help you stay on track with the change to your core context.

The most important thing for my growth was getting a coach. Someone who was on my team, who wanted my success and who was willing to work with me, be honest with me and hold me in the highest esteem so I could keep moving forward.

CHAPTER 40
WHAT IF YOU KNEW...?

Two questions I continually find refreshing are:

What if you knew you couldn't fail?

What if you knew things are as they should be?

If you consider those questions from a micro point of view, the first one is absurd. Of course, you fail – sometimes. You try something and it doesn't work. By definition, that is a failure.

What if, on the other hand, each failure is a step forward? What if a failure is just a learning point or a stepping-stone? Sometimes we say those things as temporary encouragement, hoping to distract our sadness from the feeling of not being good enough.

Since you are a divine being with a mission, gifts, and talents, then the truth is every step along the way is a learning opportunity. Whether a failure is brought on by a poor choice, circumstance, or actions of others, it still represents a learning opportunity.

The important choice is to see it that way. Anger, frustration, and blame that rage around a temporary mishap doesn't move us forward, and saps our energy and courage.

Asking, "What is the gift?" Is the key to understanding every failure is simply a lesson and instructs us not only about the goal but refines our character at the same time.

A short-term view focuses only on the immediate goal. "I wanted to make $10,000 this month. I didn't. I failed. Therefore, I suck." From the perspective of that single goal, that is a possible view.

Another view is, "That goal didn't happen this month. What can I learn? How can this change who I am in the world? If I know this is a growth opportunity and will teach me, and my heart is open to learning, what is the lesson?"

If this inquiry is conducted without drama and in the true spirit of the "Surrender Trail," then it brings peace in every circumstance. Someone once said, "pain is required, suffering is optional."

If pain is the momentary failure and suffering is continually marinating in the pain, and the self-abuse we heap on ourselves for not achieving the objective, then this quote makes a lot of sense.

The second question, "What if you knew things are as they should be?" This takes an even larger point of view.

Knowing you can't fail means if you continue on the path and make necessary adjustments, you will get to success.

Our definition of success changes throughout life. As a kid, maybe the next thing you want is ice cream. A few years later, you understand the idea of working for something over a longer horizon and choose to delay gratification.

As you mature into adulthood, you become more certain there is a much larger scheme of things at work. The accumulation of wealth and things begins to diminish in importance, and the true values in life come to the foreground.

The truth things are as they should be is not a panacea or a pat on the head. It is not an excuse for lack of effort. It's not the proverbial "there, there, it will all be okay."

Instead, it's a recognition that the combination of the "Surrender Trail," "Trusting the Divine," and a commitment to live in accordance with the four fundamental truths about who we are, absolutely provides the path of greatest fulfillment and joy.

Take some time right now and do some significant thinking and meditation on your own personal answers to the two questions at the start of this chapter. What *would* you do differently if you knew you could not fail?

What would you do differently, and how would you act differently if you *knew* things are as they should be? Setbacks and detours are temporary, and your own vision is limited by design.

Accepting these two principles and deciding how to use them is foundational to create liberation and power to shift your core context. You'll then develop a greater commitment and determination to move further and further up the "Surrender Trail."

Chapter 41
Meditation and Ritual

In all my writings and teachings, I often talk about meditation. I also refer regularly to a morning ritual. These two elements are indispensable in gathering the power to walk without fear.

I can't tell you what you must do. I can share with you what I do, how it works and what happens for clients I work with who follow these guidelines. It'll be up to you to choose whether to use them and how to use them in your quest for peace and joy.

I started meditating at age 17. It was tied to martial arts, which was a big deal for me then. Besides several meditation styles, I experimented with self-hypnosis and other tools to examine the inner world.

It was my lifeline against depression and probably the practice that kept me alive through the decades that followed. After experimentation and practice, I devised a system that works powerfully for me and created the connection to my inner wisdom, the ability to calm my mind and body at will, and the profound connection with the divine.

The first five books in my career as an author were a series about meditation. If you want to read those books, information is in the appendix. Over the years, I've distilled the practice of meditation into three steps.

1. Slow down enough to be where you are.

2. Be still enough to notice what is there.

3. Trust that what comes to you is the truth.

Our bodies fidget and our minds race. In this state of heightened activity and anxiety, we are not attentive, and we are not creative. Setting aside time to slow down physically, mentally, and spiritually is the essential first step.

Starting with just 10 minutes of stillness and quiet is a great beginning. When thoughts intrude, gently set them aside and return to the stillness. Using your breath as the focal point to start with. By using the breath, I mean, just focus on the act of breathing and feel it in your body from top to bottom.

There are hundreds of beginner courses on meditation, and they'll all work. I recommend using something simple with few requirements and no special gear or setting required. If you want a suggestion, Volume I of my meditation series *Meditation, The Amazing Journey Within,* is a great place to start.

The big key is simply to begin. Most people tell themselves they will and then don't. Another large group starts and doesn't continue. The value comes from consistency. There are dozens of free apps in all smartphone stores that can get you started as well.

You will feel frantic. You will think you can't slow down. You will feel you are doing it "wrong." All this is normal and means nothing except you are learning.

Being still is different from slowing down. Slowing down is the work required to eliminate distraction and relax physically, mentally, and spiritually. After you slow down, then you can be still enough to notice what is there.

You will become aware of feelings and thoughts unrelated to normal hectic daily routines. Noticing those things and allowing them to float in your during your slow state will produce ideas and awareness that you currently don't have.

In addition, intuition and inspiration will come to you. Calmness and focus will be their companions. Your sense of connection with the divine and the universe will expand. To be still and notice what is there will increase your creativity and decrease your worry.

Part three is to trust that what comes to you is the truth. That means to realize that in connection with the divine, there is only truth. Learning to recognize and trust intuition and inspiration is the next big step. Acting on that intuition and inspiration is the experiment that will teach you the truth.

This short explanation is not enough to get you started. Please get help and commit to creating this powerful addition to your life.

Ritual is the second part of the equation. I have a morning ritual, created, adjusted, and refined dozens of times over the years. As I teach this to clients, I have simplified it into four steps.

1. Spiritual Action.

2. Physical Action.

3. Emotional Action.

4. Mental Action.

There are lots of ways to divide up life. I use these four categories in this particular order because it is the most powerful way I have experimented with. I include the word action because thinking alone is not enough.

I complete my morning ritual without fail. I do it in the morning because it sets up the day well. It increases peace, productivity, and creativity. It has become so essential that I would no more skip the ritual than go naked to a meeting.

Spiritual Action

Spiritual action is doing something that connects to your higher power. This could be meditation, reading sacred literature, prayer, or some combination of all these things. Experiment until you find a spiritual action that activates your trust and connection to the divine.

Physical Action

Physical action acknowledges the container of your essence or the body where your spirit lives. Exercise, stretching, yoga, and any other focused action that wakes up, energizes and prepares the body for the day is sufficient. Do this even if you work out later. It is the pilot light that ignites the fire of your energy.

Emotional Action

Emotional action is acknowledging the part of life that deals with love, emotion, relationships, and the connections we have with our fellow beings. Take specific and intentional action with regard to one relationship. Send a love note, send an apology. Get creative. Don't skip this part.

Mental Action

Mental action is activating the learning, growing, and creative parts of our brain and heart. An example of mental action is reading a chapter in a book that interests you.

It could be expanding your marketing knowledge by watching a YouTube video or completing a module of a course you purchased.

My morning ritual is a minimum of 10 minutes in each of these activities. I use the acronym 'SPEM' to remind me of both the actions and the order in which they should be taken.

A simple morning ritual consists of 10 minutes focused on each area. This prepares you for the day, focuses your spirituality, intuition, and creativity, connects you to those you love and sharpens your mind for action.

These extremely brief descriptions of meditation and ritual barely scratch the surface on this topic. The purpose of this book is not to teach these in detail. Please reach out to me, or consult some of my other literature for specific instructions and processes to make those real in your life.

It's not possible to describe how powerful and effective these practices are in creating a sense of ownership, eliminating fear, and living in your true creativity and power. Only your experimentation will help you understand what I mean. More information and references are in the appendix.

All my success coaching for businesses, individuals, high performers, and superstars in every walk of life contains these two critical elements. Learning to walk without fear is one outcome of these practices.

CHAPTER 42
SURRENDER, PEACE, AND JOY

L ife is a process of learning. Some come from intentional, focused effort, learning something specific, but much comes through experience. Everything that happens to us is an opportunity to learn something. The less we learn, the faster we die.

In "Chapter 25" I introduced "The Line Of Learning" as another name for "The Surrender Trail." The learning in "Chapter 25" refers to this journey of moving through life without fear.

Here it is again for reference:

Surrender -----> Peace -----> Joy -----> Purpose -----> Power

My experience brought me to the "Surrender Trail." Founded on the four eternal truths of who we are, choices we all make about what to do with those truths, and where we are on the four threads of life, we move through this line of learning.

As soon as I understood and internalized the real meaning of intentional and joyful surrender, it produced enormous peace. No longer worried about what the future might bring, I felt at ease in every moment.

I was no longer troubled by trying to create explanations for everything in the past or frustrated by the lack of "fairness" of everything that happened around me. Trusting the divine and understanding the real purpose existence lets me both walk without fear and live in complete peace as I move through life, exercising my right to choose how I add good to the world.

The more I exercise my gifts and talents in the service of others, the happier I am. The joy of service, the joy of helping others succeed and the joy of manifesting the gifts and talents I have to accomplish the mission I accepted make life wonderful every single day.

It's a joyful game. Setbacks are challenges, disappointments are momentarily sad but swallowed up in the focus of the present. Personal challenges like the health scares I had last year are designed to increase growth and opportunity.

Living in certainty, life is happening for us, lets you be at peace and gives you the power to move forward with assurance that everything you do works for good if you choose that path.

By design, we don't see and understand everything in the present. But that fact is part of the growth process. We live the truth of faith or trust in every aspect of life.

Farmers plant, knowing that the natural processes of the earth bring forth food. We get up every day with the expectation there will be things to do and opportunities to grow.

We serve and love others in the hope and expectation that something positive will come. We do this even though there are seasons of drought where crops are destroyed, we do this even though relationships fail, and we are hit with sadness and setbacks.

We do it because we instinctively know there is a design to this whole process. All of creation is intentional, and as we learn to trust and live in that knowledge and belief, we succeed in larger and larger measures.

CHAPTER 43
WHAT'S NEXT

In the line of learning, there are five parts. This book has dealt only with the first three: "Surrender, Peace and Joy."

This is intentional. We all tend to want to rush to the endgame. Everything about our world today is designed to hurry up and get to the punchline. The creation of real development and the realization of deep joy simply does not work that way. There is no "download and double-click" solution.

Learning to walk without fear or make the most of our gifts and talents will not come from a rushed approach. Just like everything, mastering the fundamentals is critical to further success.

This book was about two things. First, sharing my experience in learning to walk without fear. I told what happened, what was revealed, gave the framework, and the exercises and practices that I used and still use every day to make life without fear.

Second, to give tools for you to experiment with and adapt for your own use.

My experience with hundreds of clients is the beautiful state of fearless creation and is available to every person.

As you explore these things and make them work in your unique situation, you are free to adapt them to your own needs and according to your circumstances. This free and fearless experimentation is key to the process.

I can promise you two things. First, if you do nothing, nothing will change. Second, if you give yourself to this pursuit, you can achieve a life without fear. This will be a life full of peace and joy where you discover, develop and manifest your own gifts and talents.

There is nothing special about me. I am a regular person who has had a set of extraordinary experiences. You have had extraordinary experiences. Your opportunity and challenge is to take those extraordinary experiences and fashion your own powerful and meaningful life, living without fear.

The next volume in this series will be *Living with Purpose and Power*. In that volume, I will describe my journey further down the line of learning moving from a place of "Surrender, Peace and Joy" into a place connecting with and enlarging my own purpose and discovering the power required to manifest it to the fullest.

This is an ongoing work which will last as long as I draw breath. This journey will be ongoing and joyful for you if you choose to walk that road. Start today and walk it with me.

I invite you to let the truths presented here sink deeply in your heart. Meditate and create your own path of discovery so that you can also walk without fear.

If you want to chat or want my help, contact information and resources are listed in the appendix.

EPILOGUE

Seven months have passed since the talk I gave in the Prologue. Once again, I found myself addressing a group of people in a setting not much different than the first occasion. During those months, I had the opportunity to explore deeply the meaning of the answer I gave in that speech.

The question was, "What is the biggest change in use since your near-death experience?" The answer, at first thought, was, "I no longer experience fear."

Since then, I have been back to the hospital and had the amazing experiences of this book. I had the opportunity to smash against the wall of uncertainty and the prospect of paralysis or death.

This new experience plunged me straight to the heart of what it means to walk without fear, not in a philosophical or hypothetical context but in the face of one more life-threatening situation.

Medical problems are obviously not the only thing that threatens life. During my decades of depression, emotional turmoil, and mental illness I felt my life threatened just as powerfully as any medical condition ever could.

At this event, I again spoke about what it means to take ownership of your life. The examples I gave were strengthened by events that happened between the two talks.

Looking at the audience, I saw reflected in the faces of those in attendance the truth that we all feel, sometimes frequently, but tend to minimize or even ignore. Each of us has something important we're prepared to do, and if we tell the truth, we really *want* to get moving.

I know why I was given these singular experiences. They were part of my development to get me to a place where I can fill the mission I agreed to. What I also know is that because of these challenges, my purpose with every breath I draw is to help *you* understand your own divinity and power.

Your walk through life will be the most joyful and productive if you choose to discover, develop, and manifest your divine nature and gifts. My deepest hope is that you will.

Learn to eliminate the noise of life. Choose to silence the monsters of fear and doubt. Listen to the true voices in your heart. Take the action they suggest. Move relentlessly forward in serving others and creating value as you add good to the world.

APPENDIX

I n my work as a coach, I am focused on helping people do things they don't believe they can do. That involves overcoming all the negative forces that convince us we are less than capable.

To that end, I have written many books which might be helpful to you. All are available on Amazon.com and from the publisher or directly from me. The books are listed below.

- *The Results Equation*
- *Meeting God at the Door*
- *The Tightrope of Depression*
- *The Book of Context*
- *Meditation, The Amazing Journey Within*
- In addition, I conduct regular workshops on topics like:
- Time Creation – Systems to Multiply Productivity
- Reading Magic – Systems to Read 10x faster than You Read Today
- Sales Systems – 4 Steps to Awesome Client Creation
- Creating Energy – Systems for Limitless Power
- Mastering Money – Understanding and Creating Wealth

I conduct 90-day goal achievement workshops called *The Results Equation Intensive*. These are designed to help you accomplish a major goal in 90 days or less. They are held "virtually" and can be attended from anywhere.

I have other kinds of coaching arrangements to help people with any situation where they are finally committed to end addiction to mediocrity and create the life of their dream.

Contact information is below, and I welcome the opportunity to get to know you.

Email Kellan at <u>CoachKellanFluckiger@gmail.com</u>

Website: www.KellanFluckiger.com

<u>www.TheResultsEquationIntensive.com</u>

ABOUT THE AUTHOR

Kellan Fluckiger is the author of the #1 best-selling books *Tightrope of Depression, The Results Equation, The Book of Context,* and *Meeting God at the Door.* He is an in-demand speaker and a highly successful coach. Working with CEOs of companies large and small, Kellan has touched and transformed many lives over the past 30 years.

A certified master coach and former C-suite Executive, Kellan has coached everyone from Super Bowl winners to BMI music award winners and everyone in between.

Kellan is a master at high achievement. As a motivational speaker and business coach, his journey has benefited thousands. He's written five books on meditation and provides coaching and support for creatives, entrepreneurs, and leaders on their journey through struggles and victories as they discover, develop, and deliver their talents to the world.

In addition to coaching, Kellan has written, recorded, and produced 11 albums of original music. He's been running a successful recording studio for over 35 years.

Samples of Kellan's music are available on his website at www.kellanfluckiger.com. You can also find his music on Amazon.

Born in San Francisco, CA, Kellan now spends most of the year creating and writing in Canada with his wife, Joy, and their two cats and dogs.